Around the World VEGAN Cookbook

FIRSTLY THANK YOU TO MY LOVELY FAMILY
AND FRIENDS - WHO ARE ALSO MY TEAM OF
LOYAL TASTE TESTERS.

AND TO ALL THE READERS OF MY BOOKS AND
WONDERFUL FOLLOWERS - THE BIGGEST THANK
YOU FOR YOUR ON-GOING SUPPORT AND LOVE.
MY RECIPES AND COOKBOOKS ARE CREATED
FOR YOU. –N.W.

Published in 2023 by Welbeck Children's Limited
part of Welbeck Publishing Group
20 Mortimer Street, London W1T 3JW
Based in London and Sydney.
www.welbeckpublishing.com

A CIP catalogue record for this book is available
from the British Library.

Author photograph p7 © Birgitta Zoutman
All other photographs © 2022 Niki Webster
Ethnic borders and patterns © Shutterstock

Author, photographer and food stylist: Niki Webster
Design Manager: Margaret Hope
Designer: Natalie Schmidt
Editor: Joff Brown
Production: Melanie Robertson

ISBN 978 1 78312 906 5

Printed in Dubai

10 9 8 7 6 5 4 3 2 1

Around the World VEGAN Cookbook

NIKI WEBSTER

WELBECK

Contents

About NIKI

Hi, I'm Niki and I'm a plant-based cook and cookbook author. Everyone has their own reasons for being vegan or choosing a plant-based diet. But for me, from a young age, I pretty much refused to eat meat. I just didn't like the taste and the thought of eating animals felt wrong to me. The key to eating vegan proved to be discovering the joy of eating and creating amazing plant based food – all focused on natural wholefoods and using seasonal ingredients.

One of the other things which really inspires me is global vegan cuisine! I was very lucky as I started travelling as a teenager, spending the entire summer in Turkey with a family when I was 14. It sparked a tremendous interest in travelling and discovering the incredible plant-based cuisines around the world.

Since then I spent an amazing six months travelling around Asia (India, Thailand, Cambodia, Vietnam, Laos & Nepal). Every day was a new culinary adventure! I followed up with some amazing trips through the Middle East, north Africa and all over Europe.

And that's where the inspiration for this book comes from – incredible vegan dishes from around the world. Everything from breakfasts and brunches, light bites, family favourites, party time, snacks and not forgetting sweet treats! Some things will be familiar and others might be new, but they're all incredibly tasty and fun to make.

Enjoy,
Niki xxx

Vegan traditions around the WORLD

You may think that plant based eating is a new thing. And it's certainly true that more and more people are now reducing their meat consumption, or adopting a vegan lifestyle.

But in fact, people around the world have abstained from meat on both religious and cultural grounds for thousands of years, and the word "vegetarian" was coined in the 1840s when the Vegetarian Society was created.

Did you know what many cultures have a long history of eating mostly plant-based foods?

Here are four examples from across the planet who have been mainly eating plant-based diets for centuries for cultural or religious reasons and have incredibly rich and inspiring culinary traditions.

INDIA
India has the largest number of vegetarians in the world – over 400 million. And has one of the most plant friendly (and delicious) cuisines.

We often link plant based eating in India to religious practices, which accounts for the large comparative percentage of the population adopting a vegetarian or vegan diet. Indian food, with the layering of spices and texture is a dream come true.

JAMAICA

The Rastafarian movement developed in Jamaica during the 1930s and the Rasta culture has many links to veganism.

"Ital" is the food celebrated by those in the Rastafarian movement – derived from the words "vital food". Ital food means it is natural and unprocessed. For a Rastafarian, it means no salt, no chemicals, no flesh, no blood, no whites (called white blood), no alcohol, no cigarettes, and no drugs. You can find plenty of delicious and fresh plant based options in Jamaica, like rice and peas and jerk jackfruit.

ETHIOPIA

The fasting traditions in the Orthodox Christian religion means that cuisine of Ethiopia and Eritrea has developed many plant-based dishes, as they're allowed within fasting periods (180–200 days of fasting per year).

Ethiopian food is absolutely delicious and lentil dishes like 'Misir Wat', a mixture of spices (Berbere) onion and garlic is one of them.

Another is 'Beyaynetu', a colourful vegetable dish arranged on a round of injera. All are healthy and delicious.

ISRAEL

Israel is very often associated with dishes like hummus and falafels – for good reason, as they are a staple and you can find them everywhere.

However, in recent years the vegan population has soared, giving rise to a plethora of vegan dishes, restaurants and cafes.

Store
CUPBOARD

What are the essentials to being confident in the kitchen? Here are my store cupboard recommendations for creating delicious vegan meals from all over the world.

FRUIT & VEG

A wide variety of colourful vegetables and fruits – seasonal if you can.

PANTRY

DRIED STUFF

Red split lentils – Perfect for making a delicious daal in 15 minutes

Puy lentils – The earthy flavour and texture is amazing. A very 'meaty' lentil, and great for bolognese or burgers

Quinoa – A complete plant-based protein – perfect for salads

Rices – White, arborio, brown, sushi

Pasta – All varieties

FLOURS

It's useful to have a variety for making pizzas, flatbreads, pancakes and breads.

Quality plain and self-raising flour and wholemeal – For fluffy flatbread or pizza bases

Buckwheat & gram flour (chickpeas) – My favourite gluten free options

Rye and spelt – Ancient grains with a nutty texture

NUTS AND SEEDS

These add crunch, texture, protein and good fats. Good to include daily.

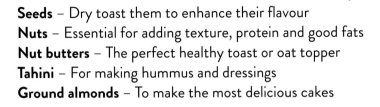

Seeds – Dry toast them to enhance their flavour
Nuts – Essential for adding texture, protein and good fats
Nut butters – The perfect healthy toast or oat topper
Tahini – For making hummus and dressings
Ground almonds – To make the most delicious cakes

CANS/JARS
Pulses including beans, chickpeas, and lentils – Keep a stock so you can make curries, chillis, dips and salads in super quick time
Tomatoes – The base for meals in minutes
Coconut milk & coconut cream – For creamy curries and decadent desserts

FRIDGE & FREEZER
FRIDGE
Milks – There are some brilliant plant-based milk in shops now – oat, almond, coconut, cashew, and soy
Cheese – Shop-bought or homemade nut cheeses
Tofu – Firm for savoury dishes, and silken to make amazing desserts
Coconut/plant based natural and greek yoghurt – Add a few tbsp to curries, soups and stews for a rich creamy texture and flavour
Vegan butter & mayo
Cream – There are some amazing vegan creams on the market now
Tomato puree

FREEZER
Frozen peas – A brilliant ingredient, for making an amazing dip/mash in minutes, and they add fantastic plant-based protein to curries
Sweetcorn/edamame/frozen veggies
Frozen fruit
Plant-based meat alternatives

Spices & Herbs

OILS

Olive oil – For cooking and roasting
Extra virgin olive oil – Adds delicious flavour for dressing, dips, and pestos
Toasted sesame oil – For adding that toasted flavour to Asian dishes
Coconut oil – I tend to use this most for Asian food
Vegetable oil – For everyday cooking and cakes

FLAVOUR ENHANCERS

Salt/Sea Salt flakes
Black Pepper
Lemon juice – Immediately enhances flavour. A squeeze of lemon can go a long way.
Stock – I absolutely love Marigold Bouillon, and it works brilliantly in soup and stews

SPICES

Indian spices – Cumin seeds, black mustard seeds, turmeric, coriander, garam masala
Mexican – Smoked paprika and ancho chilli, coriander, allspice, cloves, thyme, oregano, cinnamon, cumin
Middle Eastern – Cumin, fennel, caraway, cumin, nutmeg, cardamom, sumac, fenugreek, za'atar
European – Basil, bay leaves, celery leaves, chives, coriander (cilantro), dill tips, chervil, fennel, marjoram, oregano, rosemary, sage, tarragon, thyme
African – Berbere, ras el hanout, pul biber/aleppo pepper.
Caribbean – Allspice, ginger, cinnamon, nutmeg, cloves, garlic, paprika

For adding heat – Chilli flakes, hot paprika, cayenne
For adding sweetness – Cinnamon, ginger, allspice, mixed spice
General – Garlic powder

CONDIMENTS

Soy/Tamari – Adds savoury saltiness
Siracha – This powerful chilli sauce lets you boost meals in seconds
Rose Harissa/harissa – Adds incredible depth of flavour and colour
Nutritional Yeast – This deactivated yeast is the magic ingredient for
that nutty, cheesy, and creamy taste. It makes the perfect cheese sauce
(with cashews). It's also a great source of B vitamins

FRESH HERBS

Mint – For dips, salads and desserts
Coriander – For Asian dishes
Basil – Essential for creating batches of pesto
Spinach – A versatile leaf, perfect for salads, curries, stews, and pestos
Thyme – Brilliant in tomato dishes
Dill – Lovely in slaws and salads

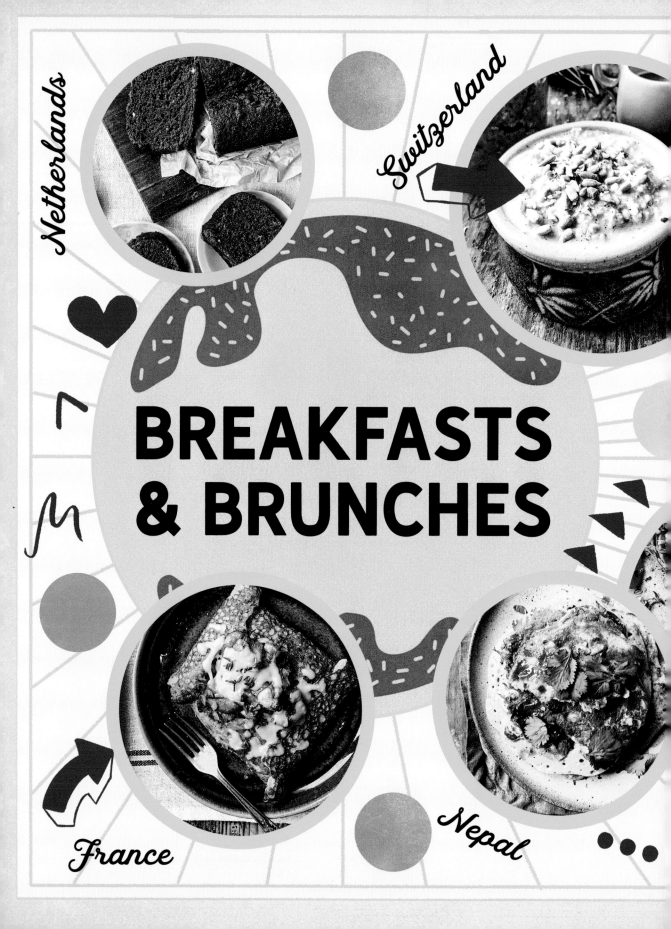

Netherlands

Switzerland

BREAKFASTS & BRUNCHES

France

Nepal

Caribbean

Uganda

Canada

USA

Australia

Difficulty – Easy
Prep – 5 minutes
Cooking – 20 minutes
Serves 2

For the roast fruit

500g (18oz) pineapple, peeled and chopped into slices

2 tbsp coconut or brown sugar

For the porridge

100g (⅔ cup) oats of choice

2 tbsp desiccated coconut

2 tbsp coconut or light brown sugar

500ml (2 cups) coconut milk drink

1 tsp vanilla extract

½ tsp ground ginger

3 large medjool dates, chopped and pitted

Toppings

2 tbsp desiccated coconut

Coconut yoghurt

Extra plant-based milk to loosen

Chopped nuts

Coconut oats with caramelised pineapple

These coconutty, creamy and lightly spiced oats are inspired by the flavours of the Caribbean. The sweet and sticky roasted pineapple is an absolutely delicious addition. Top with nutty toasted desiccated coconut for the perfect crunch.

TO ROAST THE PINEAPPLE

1. Preheat your oven to 180°C (350°F).
2. Add the pineapple to a baking tray and top with the sugar.
3. Bake for about 20–25 minutes until soft and caramelising.

TO MAKE THE PORRIDGE

1. Add the oats, milk, dates, coconut, ginger and vanilla to a small saucepan.
2. Simmer on a low heat, stirring continuously for a few minutes, until the oats are soft and have absorbed the milk but are not too dry.
3. Turn off the heat and serve with the roast pineapple, desiccated coconut, yoghurt and more plant-based milk if needed.

INGREDIENTS

Difficulty – Easy
Prep – 10 minutes
Cooking – 15 minutes
Makes 5–6

For the pancake

100g (½ cup) self-raising flour
50g (¾ cup) oat flour
½ tsp mixed spice
150ml (1/2 cup plus 2 tbsp) plant-based milk
2 tbsp vegan natural yoghurt
1 tsp vanilla extract
1 small ripe mashed banana
3 tbsp maple syrup
1 tsp baking powder
3 tbsp vegan choc chips

For the banana

2 banana sliced into slices
1 tbsp coconut oil
1 tbsp maple syrup

Toppings

Maple syrup
Natural yoghurt
Choc chips

Fluffy caramelised banana pancakes with choc chips & maple syrup

My love for caramelised bananas knows no bounds. Here I've taken the classic banana pancake combination to a new level of deliciousness with these fluffy pancakes topped with little nuggets of gooey caramelised bananas.

The delicious pancake mix includes vanilla and fragrant mixed spice, and the maple and banana add sweetness. It's a decadent breakfast or a super-speedy dessert.

TO MAKE THE BANANA PANCAKE
1. Add the flour, oat flour, spices, milk, yoghurt, vanilla, mashed up banana, choc chips, maple, and baking powder to a bowl, and mix thoroughly to combine and form a thick batter.
2. Now add 2 tbsp of the batter to a nonstick pan and fry for 1–2 minutes until the underside is firm, you should see little bubbles forming on top.
3. Carefully flip the pancake and then cook for another minute or so until the pancake is cooked through and slightly golden.
4. Repeat with all the batter

TO CARAMELISE THE BANANAS
1. Peel and slice the bananas
2. Add the coconut oil to a frying pan. Allow to melt, then add in the bananas.
3. Allow to caramelise on both sides. Flip a couple of times, then add to maple syrup to coat.

Difficulty – Easy
Serves 2
Prep – overnight

For the muesli pots
100g (2/3 cup) oats of choice
500ml (2 cups) plant-based milk
3 tbsp orange or apple juice
1 tbsp allspice
2 apples grated
½ tsp ground cinnamon
½ tsp all spice
½ tsp vanilla extract
2 tbsp seeds or nuts
1 tbsp maple syrup

Toppings optional
Fruit of choice
Nuts and seeds

Bircher muesli pots

Bircher muesli is the original overnight oats, and it was actually developed by a Swiss doctor called Dr. Maximilian Bircher-Benner for his patients at his health clinic in Switzerland.

There have been so many versions since, but I think the original including grated apple is fantastic. I've added some tasty additions: spices, vanilla, seeds and a slash of maple.

TO MAKE THE MUESLI POTS

1. Pop the oats, milk, orange juice, allspice, grated apples, spices, vanilla, maple and seeds into a container and mix well.
2. Seal the container and chill in the fridge overnight.
3. Remove from the fridge and transfer to a bowl.
4. Grate in the apple, stir and loosen if needed with a little more plant-based milk.
5. Top with toppings of choice.

INGREDIENTS

Difficulty – Easy
Serves 8–10
Prep – 10 minutes
Cooking – 35 minutes

For the banana oat and coconut bread
3 large ripe bananas, peeled
95g (½ cup, packed) light brown sugar
1 tbsp apple cider vinegar
100ml (⅓ cup plus 1 tbsp) plant-based milk
65g (1 cup) desiccated coconut
150g (1 cup) oats of choice
110g (1 cup) white plain flour or spelt flour
2 tsp baking powder
1 tsp vanilla paste or extract
½ tsp ground cinnamon

Toppings
1 banana sliced into rounds
Light brown sugar

To serve
Jam of choice – I used dark cherry
Greek style vegan yoghurt

Toasted banana oat & coconut bread

Banana bread orginates in 1930s America, and was created as an economical option. It really is one of the best ways of using up overripe bananas, as their sweetness and squidgy texture are absolutely delicious when baked. My version is next-level, as I've added some special extra ingredients like desiccated coconut, oats and sweet spices.

This addictive banana, oat and coconut bread should be toasted before topping with sweet jam and creamy yoghurt or nut butter.

TO MAKE THE BANANA OAT AND COCONUT BREAD

1. Preheat oven to 180°C (350°F). Line or grease a loaf tin.
2. Add all the ingredients to a food processor and blend until smooth.
3. Transfer the mix to to the loaf tin and smooth out the top
4. Top with the banana slices and sprinkle with brown sugar
5. Bake for 35 minutes, or until it cooked in the middle. Check by inserting a skewer into the middle.
6. Allow to cool before slicing.
7. Can eat topped with jam and yoghurt, but I love to toast it first.

Difficulty – Easy
Prep – 10 minutes
Cooking – 50 minutes

140g (1.5 cups) light rye flour
100g (¾ cup) plain flour
3 tsp baking powder
1 tsp ground cinnamon
2 tsp ground cardamom
3 tsp ground ginger
¼ tsp ground coriander
Pinch ground cloves
¼ tsp salt
130g (⅔ cup) light brown sugar
80g (¼ cup) molasses
110g (⅓ cup) golden syrup
250g (1 cup) plant-based milk

Spiced ontbijtkoek cake

An ontbijtkoek is a Dutch and Flemish spiced cake. Think of a cross between ginger cake and malt loaf, and you'll be on the right lines. It's **amazing**! It's squidgy, gingery and brilliant for breakfast, as a snack or dessert.

It's traditionally made with honey and molasses, but I've swapped the honey for golden syrup. You could use maple syrup if preferred. Its usually eaten smeared with butter – love it!

TO MAKE THE CAKE

1. Preheat the oven to 180°C (350°F) and grease and line a loaf tin with parchment paper.
2. In a large bowl, add the flours, baking powder, spices, salt and sugar and mix until combined.
3. Now add the molasses, golden syrup and milk and mix until the batter is very smooth.
4. Pour the batter into the loaf tin and bake for 50 minutes.
5. The ontbijtkoek is done when a toothpick inserted into the centre comes out clean.
6. Allow to cool completely before slicing and serving with butter.

INGREDIENTS

Difficulty – medium
Serves 2
Prep – 15 minutes
Cooking 35 minutes

For the roast tomatoes
250g (9oz) cherry
tomatoes, sliced in half
1 tbsp olive oil
Pinch sea salt and black
pepper

For the pesto
30g (⅓ cup) fresh basil
60g (⅓ cup) pine nuts
Juice ½ lemon
3 tbsp extra virgin olive oil
½ tsp sea salt
4 tbsp nutritional yeast
1 clove garlic peeled
50ml (¼ cup)water

For the dressing
½ can cooked chickpeas
drained
3 tbsp of the pesto

Charred bread
2 slices chunky bread of
choice, toasted

Toppings of choice
1 avocado, peeled and
sliced
Toasted seeds
Handful of olives
Fresh herbs of choice dill
and basil
Extra virgin olive oil

Pesto chickpeas, avocado & roast tomato toast

This is inspired by warm and sunny mornings and lazy brunches. Australia grows some of the freshest and most flavour-packed produce, and this fresh delicious toast is bursting with vibrant colour and taste. Charred fresh bread, topped with pesto chickpeas, popping roast tomatoes, avocado and fresh herbs – wonderful.

TO ROAST THE TOMATOES
Add the tomatoes, oil, salt and pepper to a baking tray and bake for about 25 minutes until soft and browning at the edges.

FOR THE PESTO
1. Firstly dry-toast the pine nuts in a small pan on a medium heat. Be careful not to burn them.
2. Add all the pesto ingredients to a food processor and blend to a chunky paste.
4. In a bowl, mix 3 tbsp of the pesto to the chickpeas. Stir to combine.

TO SERVE
1. Toast the bread on a griddle pan or in a toaster, then layer with the pesto.
2. Now top with pesto chickpeas, roast tomatoes, toasted seeds, olives, avocado and lots of fresh herbs and dollops of pesto.

Difficulty – Easy

Makes 6 medium omelettes

Prep – 10 minutes

Cooking – 35 minutes

For the filling

1 red onion, chopped up roughly

1 tsp olive oil

½ green chilli sliced

1 tsp ground turmeric

1 tsp garam masala or curry powder

200g (1.5 cups) gram flour

290g (10oz) natural silken tofu

1 tsp sea salt

1 tsp baking powder

Twist black pepper

1 tsp garlic granules

3 tbsp nutritional yeast

250ml (1 cup) water

125g (4.5oz) tomatoes chopped up roughly

10g (2 tbsp) fresh coriander (cilantro)

For the sauce

2 tbsp tamarind paste

Big pinch salt

1 tsp ground ginger

1 ½ tbsp light brown sugar

75ml (⅓ cup) water

Serve with bread

Masala chickpea omelettes

When I was trekking in Nepal, I remember the breakfasts being incredible. Big and hearty plates of lightly spiced potatoes, homemade baked beans and spiced omelettes. My masala chickpea omelettes are packed with loads of flavour from the spices, nutritional yeast for a hint of cheesiness, and fresh coriander.

Top with a slightly sweet tamarind sauce and squidge into fresh bread – delicious!

TO PREPARE THE FILLING

1. In a small pan – gently fry the onion on a medium heat until soft and browning.
2. Add the spices and chilli and cook for a further minute.
3. Turn off heat and set aside.
4. Now add the flour, tofu, garlic, nutritional yeast, and water to a blender or food processor. Blend to combine until you get a smooth batter.
5. Transfer to a large bowl, then add the cooked onion and spices, tomato and coriander (cilantro).
6. Mix to combine thoroughly.

TO COOK

1. Add a splash of oil to a non-stick frying pan then add 4 tbsp of the batter to the pan. Smooth with a spoon to distribute towards the corners of the pan.
2. Cook on a medium heat for approximately 2 minutes until there are bubbles in the chickpea omelette, and you can lift the edges up easily.
3. Flip it and cook on the other side for 1–2 minutes.
4. Repeat with the remaining mix.

TO MAKE THE SAUCE

Add the sauce ingredients to a saucepan and heat for 2–3 minutes, stirring continuously.

TO SERVE

Top the omelettes with the sauce and serve with fresh bread.

Crispy mushroom, leek & cheese galettes

INGREDIENTS

Difficulty – Medium
Makes 4 galettes
Prep – 10 minutes
Cooking – 20 minutes

For the galettes

100g (¾ cup) buckwheat flour
1 tsp of salt
1 tsp baking powder
250ml (1 cup) plant-based milk
100ml (⅓ cup plus 1 tbsp) water
1 tsp apple cider vinegar
1 tbsp olive oil

For the filling

1 large leek cleaned and sliced
1 tbsp vegan butter
1 tbsp olive oil
200g (7oz) mushrooms
2 tbsp fresh thyme leaves
Salt and black pepper

Toppings

Vegan cheese
Thyme

I remember first eating French galettes on family holidays when I was little. I felt like they were so different to anything I'd ever eaten before – even though it's just a delicious savoury crêpe. I think it was the whole experience to sitting in a French bistro which made it so special. Here they are filled with a mix of buttery caramelised leeks, mushrooms, and then topped with cheese – yum!

TO MAKE THE BATTER

1. Add the dry ingredients in a bowl. Now add the plant-based milk, water, apple cider vinegar and oil. Mix to combine well.

TO MAKE THE FILLING

1. Add the butter and olive oil to a frying pan and allow the butter to melt.
2. Now add in the leeks and fry for 7–8 minutes until soft.
3. Add the mushrooms and cook for a further 2–3 minutes until cooked.
4. Season with salt and pepper and stir in the fresh thyme.

TO MAKE THE GALETTES

1. Preheat your grill to medium. Add a little oil to a large nonstick frying pan.
2. Scoop up ½ ladle full at a time of the batter and and swirl with back of the ladle towards the edges of the pan
3. Allow to cook for a minute or so on a medium heat then add 2 tbsp of the filling to the middle of the galette.
4. Now fold each side of the crepe in towards the filling to create a square envelope shape.
5. Turn off the heat and add a little more of the filling mix to the top of the galette and then sprinkle with grated plant-based cheese.
6. Pop under the grill for 1-2 minutes so the cheese melts.
7. Repeat with the remaining batter and filling.

Difficulty – Medium
Makes 4 bagels
Prep – 15 minutes
Cooking – 15 minutes

For the tofu
1 225g (8oz) pack firm smoked tofu
2 tbsp soy sauce or tamari
2 tbsp vegan Worcestershire sauce
1 tbsp maple syrup
1 tbsp apple cider vinegar
1 tbsp smoked paprika
1 tbsp olive oil

For the charred tomatoes
200g (7oz) cherry tomatoes sliced in half
1 tbsp olive oil
1 tbsp balsamic syrup

For the pea smash
350g (2 ⅓ cups) frozen peas defrosted
Juice ½ lemon
½ tsp sea salt
2 tbsp olive oil

To serve
4 tbsp vegan mayo
Dill pickles or gerkins

4 bagels sliced in half

Breakfast bagel with smoked crispy tofu, tomatoes & pea smash

I ate the most amazing bagels for breakfast when I visited New York – soft and toasted and filled with avocado, smoked tofu and pickles. I've made a fun version with super-tasty bacony fried tofu, charred tomatoes and pea smash instead of the avocado. The taste and texture is fantastic; I could eat this every day.

TO MAKE THE TOFU
1. Add all the dressing ingredients to a tub, and mix to combine.
2. Slice the tofu into 8 slices and toss in the dressing.
3. Heat a griddle or frying pan to medium and add a little oil. Add the tofu slices and cook until they're browned and crispy on the bottom, about 2 minutes.
4. Flip and fry on the other side until crispy.
5. Remove from the heat and set aside.

TO MAKE THE CHARRED TOMATOES
1. Add the olive oil and balsamic to a small pan, then add the cherry tomatoes outside, edge down.
2. Fry for a few minutes then flip to char on the other side.

TO MAKE THE PEA SMASH
Add all the pea smash ingredients to a food processor and whizz to combine to a chunky mash.

TO SERVE
Toast the bagels then top with mayo, pea smash, tofu, charred tomatoes and pickles.

Niki's tip

The key to fluffy french toast: make sure the batter is thick and coats the bread really well.

Maple baked beans on French toast

Maple syrup is synomous with Canada, and it's one of my favourite sweeteners. Here it adds delicious subtle sweetness to the homemade baked beans. These sweet and savoury sticky beans are gorgeous on toast.

I've made them extra special here by transforming the bread into fluffy french toast – a special and delicious brunch or lunch dish.

INGREDIENTS

Difficulty – Medium
Serves 4
Prep – 10 minutes
Cooking – 15 minutes

For the maple beans

1 red onion, sliced
2 tbsp olive oil
3 cloves garlic, sliced
1 tbsp sweet paprika
2 tbsp sundried tomato purée
1 tin chopped tomatoes
1 cannelloni beans, drained
1 tbsp date molasses
2 tbsp maple syrup
1 tsp dijon mustard
1 tbsp vegan Worcestershire sauce
Salt and pepper to taste

For the French toast

4 small slices fresh bread
175ml (¾ cup) plant-based milk
80g (⅔ cup) self-raising flour
1 tsp baking powder
Pinch of sea salt
1 tsp Dijon mustard
2 tbsp nutritional yeast

A little olive oil

TO MAKE THE BEANS

1. In a large saucepan, add the olive oil and onions.
2. Fry on a medium heat for about 10 minutes until soft.
3. Now add the garlic and paprika and fry for a further minute.
4. Add the sun dried tomato paste and chopped tomatoes. Simmer for 2–3 minutes
5. How add the remaining ingredients and stir to combine.
6. Simmer for 10 minutes until thick and sticky.
7. Seasonal well.

TO MAKE THE FRENCH TOAST

1. In a bowl, whisk together the milk, flour, baking powder, mustard, nutritional yeast and salt.
2. Pour the batter into a shallow dish, then add a slice of bread and then flip to coat both sides.
3. Drizzle a little oil into a large nonstick frying pan over medium heat.
4. When the pan is hot, add the bread slices and cook for a few minutes per side, until golden brown. Repeat for the rest of the bread.

Difficulty – Medium
Makes 4
Prep – 30 minutes
Cooking – 10 minutes

4 medium chapatis
or wraps

For the vegan omelettes
300g (10.5oz) silken tofu
75g (½ cup) chickpea flour
1 tsp ground turmeric
Black pepper
1 tsp black salt (optional)
Pinch of sea salt flakes
1 tsp baking powder
200ml (¾ cup) water
1 green chilli chopped up
finely – remove the seeds
Handful of coriander
(cilantro)
½ red onion, chopped
finely
2 tomatoes, chopped
finely
½ red pepper, chopped
into small cubes
50g (¼ cup) green
cabbage, shredded

Toppings
Sriracha sauce
Vegan mayo
Fresh coriander (cilantro)

Veggie stuffed rolex

If you haven't heard of Ugandan rolex, it's a vegetable-packed omelette in a chapati wrap – a delicious street food breakfast. Traditionally it includes onion, tomato and cabbage.

My vegan version is just as packed with veg, and of course I've sneaked some spices and herbs into the 'eggy' mix. If you want to add some fire to your morning, spread sriracha over the omelette before rolling in the wrap.

TO MAKE THE VEGAN OMELETTES

1. Add the tofu, gram flour, spices, baking powder and water to a food processor. Whizz until very creamy.
2. Transfer to a large bowl then add in the chopped veg, coriander and chilli.
3. Allow to rest for 20 minutes.
4. Heat a nonstick pan to medium, then spoon a ladle of the mix at a time into the pan. Push out to the sides of the pan with a spoon.
5. Cook for 2–3 minutes until bubbles appear and the corners start to lift.
6. Heat the grill then pop the pan under to firm up the top – test the middle is cooked.
7. Remove from the grill then pop a wrap on top of the omelette.
8. Flip onto a plate to turn out.
9. Drizzle sriracha and mayonaise and add fresh coriander (cilantro).
10. Roll up up into the wrap.
11. Repeat for the rest of the mixture.

Niki's tip
The batter can be made ahead and kept in the fridge until needed.

South Africa

Spain

=

India

LIGHT
BITES

Turkey

Ukraine

Sweden

Iran

Italy

Middle East

Indonesia

Mexico

Thailand

Bunny chow with sweet potato & chickpea curry

This is such a fun way to eat curry – served in crispy bread rolls! They're the perfect edible bowls. Bunny chow originated in Durban, South Africa and it's said to have been made by the Indian 'banians' who migrated there. My version has creamy and comforting sweet potato and chickpea curry inside – absolutely delicious.

TO MAKE THE CURRY

1. Add the oil to a large pan, heat to medium then add the onions and fry for about 8 minutes until soft.
2. Add all the spices, garlic and ginger and stir to combine. Cook for 1 minute.
3. Add the chopped tomatoes and allow to break down for 2–3 minutes.
4. Add the sweet potato, coconut cream and water.
5. Cover and simmer for 15 minutes, or until the sweet potato is soft.
6. Finally, add in the chickpeas, season well and cook for a further 2 minutes.

TO SERVE

1. Cut off the top of your buns, hollow out the centres, then spoon in the curry.
2. Top with some fresh coriander (cilantro) and tuck in!

Niki's tip
You can serve this in the more traditional way if preferred: a whole hollowed-out loaf. Both are fantastic!

INGREDIENTS

Serves 4
Difficulty – Easy
Cooking – 2 minutes

4 slices rye bread

For the cashew cream cheese
200g (7oz) cashews, soaked for at least 2hrs
3 tbsp nutritional yeast
1 tsp sea salt
1 tsp smoked garlic granules
2 tbsp apple cider vinegar
50ml (¼ cup) water
3 tbsp chives, chopped

For the beetroot pickles
250g (9oz) cooked beetroots, chopped up finely
1 tbsp olive oil
1 tbsp apple cider vinegar
1 tsp maple syrup
2 tbsp fresh dill, chopped
Big pinch of sea salt

Toppings
Lots of fresh dill

Open rye sandwich with cream cheese and beetroot pickles

This is such a simple recipe inspired by tasty Swedish open sandwiches with rye bread, fresh layered toppings and lots of dill. My version? Creamy cashew cheese with fresh chives, and a super quick beetroot pickle – it's so good!

TO MAKE THE CASHEW CHEESE
Add all the ingredients to a food processor or high speed blender, and whizz until smooth and creamy.

TO MAKE THE BEETROOT PICKLES
Add all the ingredients to a bowl and toss to combine.

TO SERVE
Toast the rye bread and top with cashew cheese, beetroot pickles and fresh dill.

Niki's tip
You could try adding extra fresh garlic to the cashew cheese for a garlic cheese version.

Difficulty – Easy
Serves 4
Prep – 10 minutes
Cooking – 35 minutes

4 ciabatta rolls

For the refried beans

1 onion, chopped up

1 tbsp olive oil

2 garlic cloves, finely chopped

5 slices jalapeño

½ tsp ground cinnamon

¼ tsp ground cloves

1 can crushed tomatoes

230g (12oz) red kidney beans, rinsed and drained

2 tbsp vegan butter

1 pinch salt and freshly ground black pepper

For the roast veg

2 peppers chopped into slices

1 aubergine (eggplant) chopped into slices

1 tbsp olive oil

Pinch sea salt

Toppings

2 tbsp vegan mayo

1 avocado mashed

Pickles and herbs

Torta sandwich with roast veg & refried beans

Torta is Mexico's most popular sandwich, which has layers of tasty fillings like re-fried beans, roast veg, pickles and mayonnaise. I love adding the warm beans which makes it more substantial, but it's the layering which makes the sandwich really special.

TO MAKE THE ROAST VEG

1. Preheat your oven to 180°C (350°F).
2. Add the aubergine (eggplant) and peppers to a baking tray.
3. Drizzle with olive oil and sea salt.
4. Bake for 25–30 minutes, or until soft.

TO MAKE THE BEANS

1. Add the oil to a large pan and fry the onions for 8-9 minutes until soft.
2. Add the garlic, jalapeño, cinnamon, and cloves, and cook the mix for about 1 minute.
3. Add the tomatoes and the beans and bring to a simmer for 10 minutes.
4. Stir in the butter and season well.

TO SERVE

1. Toast the ciabatta then spread some mayonnaise on the base.
2. Top with some roast veg, refried beans, mashed avocado, pickles and herbs.
3. Place the top of the ciabatta on top.

Difficulty – Medium
Makes 8 empanadas
Prep – 20 minutes
Cooking – 40 minutes

For the dough
150g (1 ⅛ cup) plain flour
100g (¾ cup) self raising flour
½ tsp salt
½ tsp baking powder
½ tsp baking soda
2 tbsp extra virgin olive oil
150ml (⅔ cup) warm water

For the filling
1 red onion finely chopped
1 tbsp olive oil
3 cloves garlic sliced
300g (10.5oz) sweet potato
peeled and chopped into 1 cm
cubes
130g (4.5oz) cherry tomatoes
chopped
2 tbsp soy sauce
60g (2oz) sun dried tomatoes
drained and chopped
1 tsp balsamic syrup
50ml (¼ cup) water
Salt and lots black pepper
200g (7oz) firm smoked tofu
finely chopped up

For the dipping sauce
20g (⅓ cup) coriander
(cilantro) leaves
20g (⅓ cup) mint leaves
¼ tsp chili powder
6 tbsp vegan natural yoghurt
1 lime juice
1 clove garlic
¼ tsp salt

Empanadas with sweet potato & smoked tofu with aji verde

You can find empanadas in many countries, but they originated in Spain. It's a baked or fried turnover comprising pastry and filling, and delicious indeed! There are now many variations around the world – especially in Latin American countries. I remember eating them in Brazil – so good!

My version isn't very traditional as the filling is a joyous mix of flavours, including sweet potato, smoked tofu and sun-dried tomatoes. I've accompanied it with a zingy Peruvian green sauce (aji verde) which I think works perfectly.

TO MAKE THE DOUGH
1. Add the flour, salt, baking powder and baking soda to a large bowl.
2. Stir to combine, and then add in the oil and warm water.
3. Mix to combine well, and transfer to a floured surface.
4. Knead the dough until it becomes springy.
5. Pop it back in the bowl and drizzle with a little olive oil until after you've made the filling mix.

TO MAKE THE FILLING
1. Add the oil to a medium saucepan and heat to medium, then add the onion.
2. Fry for 8–10 minutes until soft.
3. Now add the garlic and sweet potato and fry for 3–4 minutes. Stirring frequently.
4. Add the tomatoes, soy sauce, sundried tomatoes, balsamic and water. Stir and cover for 5 minutes.
5. Add chopped tofu and salt and black pepper
6. Cover and simmer for 5 more minutes.

TO MAKE THE EMPANADAS

1. Form the dough into a ball and divide into 8 equal sections.
2. Preheat a large frying pan or griddle. Add a little oil.
3. Roll each section into a ball and flatten out onto a lightly floured surface. Use a rolling pin to help roll the balls out to about 15cm diameter circles.
4. Now scoop up about 2 tbsp of the filling and pop in the centre of each dough.
5. Fold over the filling to make a crescent shape. Press down the outer edges so that you get a good seal, and press a fork around the outer edges.
6. Add two empanadas to the pan and cook for a few minutes until golden brown, then flip over and cook the other side.
7. Remove from the pan.
8. Repeat with the remaining dough and mix.

TO MAKE THE SAUCE

1. Add all the ingredients to a food processor and blend until smooth.
2. Serve the empanadas with the dipping sauce.

INGREDIENTS

Difficulty – Medium
Makes about 10
Prep – 15 minutes
Cooking – 30 minutes

For the tofu

1 can black beans, drained
and rinsed
1 tbsp smoked paprika
1 tsp ground cumin
1 tsp oregano
1 tsp garlic granules
3 tbsp nutritional yeast
4 tbsp sun dried tomato puree
3 tbsp soy sauce
3 tbsp balsamic vinegar
Pinch sea salt and black
pepper
1 400g (14oz) pack firm tofu
drained and cut into small
cubes
Handful of fresh mint and
coriander (cilantro)

For the mango salsa

1 large ripe mango peeled and
sliced into cubes
Fresh coriander (cilantro) &
mint shredded
150g (5oz) cherry tomatoes
sliced
Juice ½ lime
1 tbsp olive oil
Pinch sea salt flakes and chilli
flakes

1 pack of 10 corn tacos

Toppings

Fresh mint
1 avocado, chopped
Natural yoghurt /mayonnaise
Squeeze lime juice

Spiced black bean tofu & mango salsa tacos

This is one for all you spicy Mexican flavour lovers!
Baking the black bean tofu mix means the flavours
get cooked into the mix to intensify the flavours.
Once you've loaded your taco with the tasty black
bean mix, top with some fresh and fruit mango salsa,
creamy mayo and avocado – wonderful.

TO MAKE THE FILLING

1. Preheat your oven to 180°C (350°F).
2. In a large bowl, add all the ingredients apart from the tofu and mix to combine.
3. Now add the tofu and mix gently again to combine.
4. Line a large baking tray with baking paper then spread out the mix.
5. Bake for 30 minutes.
6. Set aside to cool, then stir in the fresh mint and coriander (cilantro).

TO MAKE THE SALSA

Add all the ingredients to a small bowl and mix to combine.

TO SERVE

1. Heat a frying pan to medium, then add the corn tacos to the pan until they warm through on each side.
2. Transfer to a serving platter and then top with the tofu mix, salsa, avocado lots of fresh mint, lime and dollops of natural yoghurt.

INGREDIENTS

Difficulty – Advanced
Makes 2 medium pizzas
Prep – 15 minutes
Cooking – 2 hrs, including
bread resting phase

For the dough

250g (2 cups) strong white
bread flour, plus extra to dust

½ tsp salt

7g fast-action dried yeast

1½ tsp caster sugar

75ml (3 tbsp) vegetable oil,
plus extra for oiling

100ml (⅓ cup plus 1 tbsp)
lukewarm water

For the topping

1 red onion chopped roughly

2 tbsp olive oil

3 cloves garlic

1 tsp cumin seeds

1 tbsp smoked paprika

1 red pepper chopped up
finely

300g (10.5oz) mushrooms
chopped up very finely

3 tsp sun friend tomato pure

1 tbsp pomegranate molasses

30g (⅓ cup) fresh mint
shredded

1 tbsp za'atar

Salt & pepper

Toppings

½ red onion thinly sliced

2 tbsp za'atar

2 tbsp pomegranate molasses

Fresh coriander (cilantro) or
mint finely chopped

Natural vegan yoghurt

Pine nuts

Spiced mushroom lahmacun

At the age of 14 I spent the whole summer in
Turkey, travelling around with a Turkish family and
a school friend. It opened my eyes to new tastes
and flavours, and I've never looked back. One of
my favourites things to eat was lahmacun and pides
– Turkish pizzas! I've topped my lahmacun with a
delicious mushroom topping and lots of amazing
extras like za'atar, herbs and pine nuts.

TO MAKE THE DOUGH

1. In a large bowl, mix the flour, salt, yeast and sugar.
2. Mix the oil, and water in a jug, then stir into the dry
   ingredients and bring together to form a dough.
3. Transfer onto a floured surface and knead for a few
   minutes until the dough becomes smooth and springy.
4. Pop back into the bowl and cover with a clean tea towel
   and leave to rise for 1 hour.

TO MAKE THE TOPPING

1. Add the oil to a large frying pan and heat to medium.
2. Now add the onion and fry for 8 minutes until soft.
3. Add the spices, garlic and pepper. Sauté for 3 minutes.
4. Add chopped mushrooms and tomato paste and stir everything together and sauté for another 4–5 minutes until everything is soft.
5. Add the pomegranate molasses, mint and za'atar and stir everything together.
6. Continue cooking for another minute or so then season with salt and pepper.

TO COOK

1. Preheat oven to 180°C (350°F), and line two large baking trays with baking paper.
2. Transfer the dough back onto a floured surface. Knead again, form the dough into a ball, then divide into two.
3. Roll out each piece of dough onto a oval shapes, then pop onto the lined baking trays.
4. Top with the mushroom mix. Smooth out to the corners.
5. Bake for 15–20 minutes until the base is crispy.
6. Top with sliced red onion, herbs, za'atar, yoghurt, and a drizzle of pomegranate molasses.

Niki's tip
You can make a quick version using shop-bought pizza dough, or pop the toppings on pitta breads.

INGREDIENTS

Difficulty – Easy
Seves 4
Prep – 10 minutes
Cooking – 20 minutes

For the kheema

1 red onion, peeled and finely diced
1 tbsp vegan butter
1 thumb fresh ginger, peeled and grated
4 garlic cloves, sliced
½ tsp chilli powder
200g (7oz) soy mince
1 tsp garam masala
1 tsp cumin seeds
1 tsp ground coriander
1 tsp ground turmeric
1 tsp sea salt
10 sun dried tomatoes in oil, drained and chopped
75ml (⅓ cup) water
250g (9oz) frozen peas
15g (¼ cup) mint leaves, finely chopped
15g (¼ cup) fresh coriander, finely chopped
Big pinch sea salt
Juice ½ lime

For the pav

4 bread rolls
1 red onion, peeled and very finely chopped
Lime wedges

Kheema pea pav

Kheema pav is a very popular Indian street food for good reason. It's the tastiest spiced mince (soy in this case) cooked in spices, butter and fresh herbs, then squished into toasted buttered rolls and topped with onions and a squeeze of lime. It's absolutely delicious!

TO MAKE THE KHEEMA PAV

1. In a frying pan, add the butter and red onion to a pan and fry for 10 minutes until soft.
2. Now add the ginger, garlic and chilli powder. Stir to combine.
3. Add the spices and soy mince and fry for 5 minutes.
4. Add the sun-dried tomatoes and water, and cover and cook for 2–4 minutes. Stir occasionally.
5. Now add the peas, mint, coriander (cilantro) and cook for 2 minutes.
6. Finally add the butter, lime juice and salt and mash everything up a bit.

TO SERVE

1. Toast the bread rolls and butter if you like.
2. Load the rolls with the kheema, red onion and a squeeze of lime.

INGREDIENTS

Difficulty – Medium
Serves 4
Prep – 15 minutes
Cooking – 30 minutes

For the harissa veggies

1 red pepper chopped up into small cubes
1 courgette (zucchini) chopped up into small cubes
1 small aubergine (eggplant) chopped up into small cubes
1 tbsp harissa spice mix
½ tsp cumin seeds
½ tsp sea salt
2 tbsp olive oil

For the beetroot borani

300g (10.5oz) cooked beetroots drained
1 clove garlic
2 tbsp extra virgin olive oil
3 tbsp vegan Greek style yoghurt
1½ tbsp red wine vinegar
1 tsp sea salt
Chilli flakes

For the flatbread

150g (1 ⅛ cup) self raising flour
1 tsp baking powder
Pinch sea salt flakes
75ml (⅓ cup) water
2 tbsp plant-based yoghurt

Optional additional toppings

Fresh herbs – dill, mint
Toasted pine nuts
Extra virgin olive oil
Chilli flakes

Roast harissa veggies on beetroot borani

Beetroot borani is an amazingly vibrant Iranian yoghurt dip. Made here with the creamiest vegan Greek style yoghurt, it's delicious! And it's made even better with harissa spiced roast veg and scooped with fluffy flatbreads. I challenge even beetroot avoiders not to like this one.

TO ROAST THE VEG

1. Preheat your oven to 180°C (350°F).
2. Chop the peppers, aubergine (eggplant) and courgette (zucchini) into small cubes.
3. Add the veg along with the spices and oil to a large baking tray and toss to combine.
4. Bake for about 30 minutes until soft.

TO MAKE THE DIP

1. Add the beetroot and all the ingredients into the food processor.
2. Whizz until smooth and creamy.

TO MAKE THE FLATBREADS

1. In a large bowl, add the flour and salt. Stir to combine.
2. Now add the water and yoghurt, mix thourougly to combine, and then transfer to a floured board. If you need to add a bit more water or flour, then do so.
3. Knead for a few minutes, until you get a soft and springy dough.
4. Divide the dough into 4 and roll out each piece with a rolling pin.
5. Heat a frying pan or griddle to medium and then add the the first flatbread dough. Cook on each side for 2–3 minutes until fluffy and a little charred.
6. Repeat.

TO SERVE

1. Serve the borani topped with the vegetables and additional toppings.
2. Use the flatbreads to scoop up.

INGREDIENTS

Difficulty – Easy
Serves 2–4
Prep – 15 minutes

For the salad

200g (7oz) white cabbage, shredded

1 large carrot, shredded

½ pepper, sliced

3 spring onions, sliced

4 tbsp roasted salted peanuts

20g (⅓ cup) coriander (cilantro), chopped

2 tbsp toasted sesame seeds

1 ripe mango peeled and cut into slices

1 avocado, sliced

For the peanut dressing

2 tbsp peanut butter

2 tsp rice wine vinegar

1 tsp garlic granules

½ inch piece ginger grated

2 tbsp soy sauce

1.5 tbsp sriracha

Juice 1 lime

1 tsp maple syrup

50ml (¼ cup) water

Sunshine salad with avocado, mango & peanut dressing

Thinking of Thailand gets me dreaming of sunshine, fragrant curries, and fresh and vibrant salads. Thai food has some of the most incredible flavours. This salad sings with freshness – juicy ripe mango, creamy avocado, crunchy roast peanuts, and the most amazing satay peanut sauce. Yes, it's a salad – but it's absolutely packed with flavour.

TO MAKE THE SALAD

1. Finely slice the cabbage and carrots then add to a large bowl.
2. Now add the chopped peppers, spring onions and coriander (cilantro).
3. Toss to combine, then add in the toasted seeds and peanuts.

TO MAKE THE DRESSING

Add all the ingredients to a jar and mix to combine.

TO SERVE

1. Divide the salad onto plates, then either drizzle the dressing over or toss to combine .
2. Top with the sliced avocado and mango.

Difficulty – Medium
Serves 4
Prep – 15 minutes
Cooking – 30 minutes

For the roast veg

2 corn on the cob
1 courgette (zucchini) chopped
into large cubes
1 pepper sliced roughly
1 tbsp olive oil
Pinch sea salt

For the roast tomato salsa

300g (10.5oz) cherry tomatoes
1 red onion, peeled and sliced
4 cloves garlic, peeled
1 tbsp olive oil
Pinch sea salt

Other salsa ingredients

1 tsp cumin seeds
3 handfuls mint and coriander (cilantro) leaves
1½ tbsp lime juice
1 tsp smoked paprika
½ tsp salt
Pinch chilli flakes

For the salad

1 can black beans, drained
1 tsp sea salt flakes
20g (⅓ cup) fresh mint shredded
Chilli flakes

Roast corn, veg and & tomato salad

This bright and summery Mexican-inspired bean and veg salad is healthy and packed with flavour. The roast tomato salsa dressing is fresh, super-tasty and a little spicy, and it pairs perfectly with the slightly charred sweetcorn and roast veg.

Serve with fluffy flatbreads or fresh bread – delicious!

TO ROAST THE VEG

1. Preheat your oven to 180°C (350°F).
2. Remove the corn kernels by running a knife along the core. Add to a baking tray.
3. Chop the veg and add the baking tray, drizzle with olive oil, and sprinkle with salt.
4. Roast for 30 minutes until soft and slightly charred. Remove from the oven.

TO MAKE THE SALSA

1. At the same time, add the tomatoes, onion and garlic for the salsa to another tray, drizzle with olive oil and sprinkle with salt.
2. Roast for about 30 minutes. Set aside to cool a little.
3. Now add to a food processor with the olive oil and salt and whizz briefly until you have a chunky salsa.

TO COMPILE

1. Add the roast veg, beans and mint to a large bowl.
2. Stir in the salsa.
3. Top with chilli flakes and salt.

Difficulty – Easy
Serves 4–6
Prep – 15 minutes
Cooking – 40 minutes

For the ribollita

2 tbsp olive oil
1 large onion, finely chopped
1 large carrot, finely chopped
2 celery, finely chopped
4 garlic cloves, sliced
1 can tomatoes
1 tsp sea salt
500ml (2 cups) water
1 tbsp red wine vinegar
½ tsp chili flakes
400g (14oz) can cannolini beans, drained
2 handfuls trimmed kale
3 slices crusty bread torn into chunks
Drizzle olive oil

For the cashew parmesan

50g (2oz) cashews
2 tbsp nutritional yeast
¼ tsp garlic granules
Pinch sea salt

Ribollita stew

Ribollita is a delicious Tuscan bread soup or stew made with vegetables, beans, and bread. It has lovely rich flavours and is a brilliant way of using up slightly stale bread. It's cooked in a saucepan and then transferred to the oven once topped with bread, which crisps up.

I've added some tasty cashew parmesan to the topping, which adds a lovely cheesy touch. It's healthy and delicious!

TO MAKE THE CASHEW PARMESAN
Add all the ingredients to a blender and whizz to a chunky crumb.

TO MAKE THE RIBOLLITA
1. In a large pan, add the onion, carrots, celery and oil, and fry on a medium heat for 8–10 minutes until soft.
2. Add the garlic and cook for a further 1 minute.
3. Now add the tinned tomatoes and salt to the pan, and simmer for about 8 minutes.
4. You can now add the beans, chilli flakes, red wine vinegar and 500ml (2 cups) water.
5. Bring to a simmer then add the kale and allow to soften.
6. Add 1 slice of bread, broken up, to the stew and simmer for 2–3 minutes.
7. Preheat your oven to 180°C (350°F).
8. Remove the pan from heat and transfer the mix to a casserole dish.
9. Place the remaining torn bread chunks on top of stew. Drizzle generously with olive oil and 4 tbsp of cashew parmesan.
10. Transfer to the oven and bake for around 10–15 minutes. The bread should be golden brown on top.
11. Ladle the stew into bowls to serve.

Difficulty – Easy
Serves 4
Prep – 1 hr
Cooking – 15 minutes

For the crispy tofu
400g (14oz) firm tofu
1 tbsp rapeseed oil

For the dressing
2 tbsp tamari or soy sauce
2 tbsp toasted sesame oil
1 tbsp rice vinegar
1 tbsp maple syrup
1 tbsp sriracha

For the peanut sauce
4 tbsp peanut butter
3 tbsp tamari
1 tbsp maple syrup
½ lime juice
1 tsp tamarind paste
1 tbsp sriracha
½ garlic powder
3 tbsp coconut milk or
2 tbsp of cream or vegan yoghurt
2 tbsp toasted sesame oil
50ml (¼ cup) water

For the salad;
1 large carrot, grated
1 cucumber, sliced
½ cabbage, shredded

Toppings;
4 tbsp roasted peanuts
Handful of coriander (cilantro)
Pinch of chilli flakes

Gado gado crispy tofu salad

Gado gado, the delicious Indonesian salad served with peanut sauce and tofu, is my kind of healthy food. It's packed with fresh veg, marinated crispy tofu, and the most delicious peanut satay sauce. The crispy tofu adds the most amazing flavour and texture combination.

FOR THE TOFU

1. Add all the tofu dressing ingredients to a large tub, mix to combine.
2. Slice the tofu into large cubes. Transfer to the tub, put the lid on and shake to combine.
3. Allow to marinate for at least 30 minutes – ideally a few hrs.
4. Heat the oil in a large frying pan or wok. Fry the tofu for a few mins each side until brown and crispy, then transfer to a plate.

TO MAKE THE PEANUT SAUCE

Add all the ingredients to a Mason jar. Replace the lid and shake to combine.

TO SERVE

1. Divide the salad and tofu into 4 small bowls.
2. Top with the peanut sauce, roasted peanuts and fresh coriander (cilantro).

INGREDIENTS

Difficulty – Easy
Serves 4
Prep – 15 minutes
Cooking – 20 minutes

For the soup

2 tbsp olive oil
1 onion, chopped up roughly
1 tsp cumin seeds
1 tsp black mustard seeds
1 tsp garam masala
1 tsp ground turmeric
¼–½ tsp cayenne pepper
3 cloves garlic, sliced
2 small carrots, chopped up finely
1 can crushed tomatoes
350ml (1 ½ cups) veg stock
Pinch sugar
½ tsp sea salt
Black pepper
75ml (⅓ cup) coconut milk

For the coriander mint chutney

4 tbsp vegan natural yoghurt
½ fresh lemon juice
30g (½ cup) fresh coriander (cilantro)
20g (⅓ cup) mint leaves
½ red chilli, sliced and seeds removed
2 tsp grated ginger
1 garlic clove
1½ tsp sea salt and black pepper
Pinch of sugar

Spiced tomato soup with coriander (cilantro) mint chutney

I remember eating simple spiced tomato soup many times in India – it's similar to the European version but enhanced with lovely warming spices. I've added a little coconut milk for creaminess.

It's great on its own, but even more delicious with some creamy, herby and zingy coriander (cilantro) mint chutney.

TO MAKE THE SOUP

1. Add chopped onions to a saucepan and fry for 8–10 minutes.
2. Add the spices, garlic and the carrot and cook for 4 to 5 minutes, stirring occasionally.
3. Add the onion mixture to a blender, along with the tomatoes and blend until puréed.
4. Transfer the pureed tomato mixture back to the saucepan.
5. Add stock, salt and sugar and cook over medium heat for 10 minutes covered.
6. Stir in the coconut milk and season well.

TO MAKE THE CHUTNEY

Blend all ingredients in a blender or food processor until relatively smooth.

TO SERVE

Top the soup with the coriander (cilantro) mint chutney.

Difficulty – Medium

Serves 9

Prep – 2½ hrs with resting time

Cooking – 20 minutes

For the bread

120ml (½ cup) warm water

1 tsp sugar

7g active dry yeast

450g (3 ⅓ cups) plain flour

1½ tsp salt

150ml (½ cup plus 2 tbsp) plant-based milk

3 tbsp melted vegan butter

Topping

4 tbsp olive oil

4 tbsp chopped fresh dill

5 cloves garlic, minced

Pinch of sea salt

Pampushka bread

These delicious pull-apart garlic rolls called 'pampushki' are traditional in Ukraine. Fluffy and beautifully drizzled with a garlic and herb sauce, they're incredibly moreish and great for dipping in soup or scooping up hummus. The perfect sharing bread!

TO MAKE THE BREAD

1. In a jug, combine the warm water, sugar and active dry yeast. Set aside for 10 minutes or until foamy.
2. In a large bowl, mix together the flour and salt.
3. Add the yeast mixture, milk and melted butter to the flour.
4. Mix until it forms into a dough, and transfer to a floured surface. Knead until springy.
5. Form into a ball and place back in the bowl. Cover and set aside in a warm space for about one hour, or until it doubles in size.
6. Transfer back to a floured surface and knead again for a few minutes.
7. Divide into 9 pieces and roll each piece into a ball.
8. Place the pampushki in a greased, loose-bottomed cake tin, with the first ball in the centre and then the others around it.
9. Cover with a kitchen towel. Set aside in a warm space for 30 minutes.
10. Preheat the oven to 200°C (400°F).
11. Now brush the pampushki with milk and bake for 20 minutes until golden brown.
12. In the meantime, add all the topping ingredients to a jar and mix to combine.
13. Spoon the topping over the pampushki immediately to allow it to absorb into the bread.

FAMILY FAVOURITES

Japan

Cuba

Italy

India

Sri Lanka

Greece

Mauritius

West Africa

Morocco

Asia

America

Spain

England

Difficulty – Medium
Serves 6
Prep – 15 minutes
Cooking – 1 hr

For the vegetable layers
2 small aubergines (eggplants), sliced lengthways
2 medium courgettes (zucchinis), sliced lengthways

For the sauce
2 tbsp olive oil
1 red onion, roughly sliced
3 cloves garlic, chopped
1 tbsp smoked paprika
1 tsp cumin seeds
1 red pepper, chopped
1 400g (14oz) tin chopped tomatoes
8 sun dried tomatoes, drained and chopped
2 tbsp sun dried tomato paste
100g (⅓ cup plus 1 tbsp) veg stock
250g (9oz) pre cooked puy lentils
20g (⅓ cup) fresh mint leaves, shredded
Sea salt and black pepper

For the cheesy béchamel sauce;
2 tbsp vegan butter
2 tbsp plain flour
500ml (2 cups) almond milk
3–4 tbsp nutritional yeast
1 tsp garlic powder
Big pinch of sea salt
Twist black pepper

Toppings
4 tbsp grated cheese

Spiced layered lentil & cheese bake

I remember many wonderful holidays to Greece as a little girl, and of course we ate lots of moussaka. My version has a few changes, so not strictly a moussaka – firstly it's vegan, obviously, but I've also omitted the potatoes in favour of courgettes (zucchinis). But it still has the other classic ingredients: aubergine (eggplant), a rich sauce with spices and a thick layer of cheesy sauce.

This is a lovely comforting family meal, packed with summery flavours.

TO FRY THE VEG
1. Add a portion of the veg to a frying pan or griddle with a little oil. Heat to medium and fry for 5 minutes, turning frequently.
2. Repeat with all the veg and set aside.

TO MAKE THE SAUCE
1. Add some olive oil to a large pan and heat to medium.
2. Fry the onions for 8–10 minutes until soft.
3. Next, add in the garlic and spices. Stir and cook for a further minute.
4. Add the red pepper and cook for 2 minutes until a little soft.
5. Add the remaining ingredients apart from the mint and seasonings and cook simmer gently for 10 minutes .
6. Finally stir in the fresh mint and season to taste.

FOR THE CHEESE SAUCE
1. Add the butter to a frying pan and melt on a low heat then add the flour. Stir to combine well.
2. Next add the almond milk and nutritional yeast. Simmer

for 5 minutes, stirring constantly to ensure no lumps form. Season well and remove from the heat.

TO MAKE THE BAKE

1. Preheat your oven to 180°C (350°F).

2. Using a medium rectangle or square casserole dish, firstly layer the aubergine (eggplant) along the base, then add half the lentil mix.

3. Now place the courgette (zucchini) layered over then spoon half cheese sauce over the top.

4. Now add the rest of the lentil mix, and the remaining aubergine (eggplant) and courgette (zucchini) You can alternate them.

5. And finally a layer of the remaining cheese sauce. Smooth out to cover the veg.

6. Sprinkle the vegan cheese over the top, and then bake for 40 minutes.

7. The top should be a little brown and crispy.

INGREDIENTS

Serves 4
Difficulty – Advanced
Prep – 20 minutes
Cooking – 45 minutes

For the curry sauce
2 tbsp olive oil
1 onion, roughly chopped
2 medium carrots chopped finely
4 cloves garlic sliced
Knob of ginger, grated
1 tsp ground turmeric
2 tsp curry powder
1 tbsp soy sauce or tamari
1 tbsp rice vinegar
1 tbsp white miso paste
½ tsp chilli flakes
250ml (1 cup) oat milk
250ml (1 cup) veg stock

For the curry
1 courgette (zucchini) sliced into 14–16 pieces
I pack firm tofu sliced into triangles – 16 pieces

For the batter
140g (1 ⅛ cup) plain flour
1 tbsp vegetable oil
200ml (¾ cup) water

For the crumb
100g (2 cups) panko breadcrumbs
Pinch of chilli Flakes
3 tbsp sesame seeds
1 tsp garlic granules
Pinch of sea salt

Flour dip
75g (½ cup) plain flour
Vegetable oil for frying

To serve
250g (9oz) cooked rice
Dill pickles

Tofu & courgette katsu curry

Katsu means 'cutlet' in Japanese . Here the tofu and courgette (zucchini) are 'Katsu-ed' in panko bread crumbs. It's absolutely delicious – soft inside and crispy-crunchy on the outside. The katsu curry sauce has Indian spices, but has a very mild and distinctive flavour with the addition of the soy and miso.

The result is so delicious and very moreish!

TO MAKE THE SAUCE
1. Add the oil to a large pan and heat to a low to medium heat, add in the onion. Fry for about 8–10 minutes until soft and browning.
2. Add in the carrot and cook for 2–3 minutes.
3. Now add the garlic and ginger and stir for another minute.
4. Add in the spices and stir to combine.
5. Now add the oat milk and the remaining ingredients, and cook covered until the carrot is tender – about 10 minutes.
6. Blitz until creamy with a hand blender.

TO MAKE THE KATSU
1. Firstly make the batter by mixing the flour, veg oil and water in a bowl to make it a pancake batter style consistency.
2. In another bowl, add the panko breadcrumbs, sesame seeds, chilli flakes & garlic powder. Mix to combine.
3. Add the plain flour to a third bowl.

TO COOK
1. In batches, dip the tofu and courgette (zucchini) in the flour, then the batter, then finally in the breadcrumbs.
2. Add some oil to a frying pan and heat to medium.
3. Make sure the tofu and courgette (zucchini) are really well coated, then place in the pan.
4. Shallow fry for around 2–3 minutes on each side – or until the breadcrumbs are golden.
5. Set aside and repeat with all the veg and tofu.

TO SERVE
Serve the curry with the rice, katsu tofu and courgette (zucchini) and dill pickles.

Difficulty – Easy
Serves 2–4
Prep – 10 minutes
Cooking – 25 minutes

For the dal
200g (7oz) red split
lentils, rinsed well
450ml (2 cups) water
300ml (1 ¼ cups) coconut
milk
1 tsp ground turmeric
10 cherry tomatoes
chopped in half
1 tsp salt

For the tarka
3 tbsp coconut oil
1 tsp black mustard seeds
10 curry leaves
1 tsp cumin seeds
2 red onions chopped
into slices
1 tsp grated ginger
4 large garlic cloves sliced
½ tsp chilli flakes
1 tsp coriander powder
½ tsp sea salt

Topping
4 tbsp toasted desiccated
coconut

Serve with flatbreads

Comforting dal curry

This simple and delicious dal is a Sri Lankan staple and is typically eaten with roti, rice or curry. I love the addition of coconut milk as it makes the lentils extra creamy and special.

What is tarka? It's the process of frying a bunch of spices in oil, using spices which begin to pop and sizzle, releasing that gorgeous aroma and flavour.

TO MAKE THE DAL

1. Add the lentils to a medium saucepan with 450ml (2 cups) of water. Bring to the boil and skim off the froth and add the turmeric and coconut milk.
2. Reduce to a low heat and simmer for 15 minutes.
3. Next add the tomatoes and salt.
4. Simmer for another 5 minutes, then turn off the heat.

TO MAKE THE TARKA

1. Heat the oil in a small frying pan, then add the add the mustard seeds, curry leaves and cumin.
2. When the seeds pop, add the onion.
3. Fry on a low heat until the onion is soft and caramelising – around 10 minutes.
4. Add the ginger, garlic, chilli, salt and coriander and fry for 2 minutes.

TO SERVE THE DAL

1. Stir half the tarka into the dal.
2. Top with the remaining tarka and toasted coconut.

Tip to serve
Flatbreads – see
page 113

INGREDIENTS

Difficulty – Medium
Serves 4
Prep – 15 minutes
Cooking 1 hour

1 medium cauliflower,
leaves removed.
1 tbsp garam masala
1 tsp smoked paprika
½ tsp sea salt
Olive oil to drizzle

For the sauce
2 tbsp olive oil
1 red large onion, finely
chopped
1 tsp cumin seeds
1 tsp black mustard seeds
½ tsp fenugreek
1 tsp sweet paprika
½ tsp cinnamon
3 garlic cloves, peeled and
sliced
3 tbsp sun dried tomato
paste or tomato purée
40g (1.5oz) ground
almonds
1 400g (14oz) can
tomatoes
75ml (⅓ cup) water
Salt & pepper and chilli
flakes

Whole roast cauliflower with tomato masala sauce, & cucumber mint dressing

This beautiful whole roast spiced cauliflower with creamy masala sauce is a really special dish. It's full of lovely Indian flavours, and the cauliflower is soft on the inside and crispy and spiced on the outside.

It's perfectly delicious with just the cauliflower and sauce, but it's even better with the cool and creamy cucumber mint dip dolloped around the outside. You can eat on its own or serve with rice or flatbread.

TO COOK THE CAULIFLOWER

1. Take the leaves and base off the cauliflower and score a cross in the base with a knife.
2. Add the cauliflower upside down to a large pan of boiling water. Make sure it's submerged, cover with a lid and boil for about 7 minutes – until just tender.
3. Drain and pat dry, then add it to a lined small baking tray.
4. Rub with the garam masala, smoked paprika and sea salt.
5. Drizzle all over with olive oil.
6. Bake for 45 minutes .The cauliflower should be a little crispy on the outside.

TO MAKE THE SAUCE

1. Heat the oil in a large pan with a lid.
2. Cook the onions for 10 mins over a medium heat until soft and browning.
3. Add the spices and garlic and cook for 1 minute. Stir in the tomato purée, ground almonds, water and tomatoes.
4. Bring to a low simmer, then cook covered for 15 minutes until you have a thick sauce.
5. Turn off the heat and blitz with an an immersion blender until smooth.
6. Season well and stir in the yoghurt.

2–3 tbsp vegan cream or yoghurt

Cucumber mint dip

½ cucumber grated

4 tbsp plant-based yoghurt

3 tbsp chopped fresh mint

Juice ½ lemon

½ tsp sea Salt

Twist black Pepper

1 tbsp extra virgin olive oil

Toppings;

Fresh herbs; mint, coriander (cilantro)

chilli flakes

TO MAKE THE CUCUMBER DIP

1. Grate the cucumber and pop it into a large seize to drain over a bowl. Squeeze out as much moisture as possible then transfer to a large bowl.
2. Add all the other ingredients and mix well.
3. Drizzle olive oil on top.

TO SERVE

Add the masala sauce to a serving dish, top with the cauliflower, and dollop on some cucumber mint dip.

INGREDIENTS

Difficulty – Easy
Serves 2–4
Prep – 10 minutes
Cooking – 30 minutes

2 tbsp olive oil

1 large onion, chopped roughly

1 red and 1 green pepper, chopped up finely

3 cloves garlic, sliced

450g (16oz) mushrooms, sliced

50ml (¼ cup) dry white wine or 2 tbsp white wine vinegar

2 tsp sweet paprika

1 tbsp oregano

1 tsp ground cumin

1 tbsp soy sauce

½ tsp cayenne pepper or chilli powder

1 tin tomatoes

2 bay leaves

100g (3.5oz) pimiento-stuffed Spanish olives, halved

1 tbsp white wine vinegar

Twist black pepper and salt

For the rice

250g (9oz) cooked rice

1 can black beans, drained

½ tsp sea salt

1 tbsp olive oil

Juice of ½ lime

Topping

Spring onions, sliced

Mushroom ropa vieja with rice & black beans

Ropa Vieja is a tasty Cuban dish – traditionally made with beef, peppers and pimiento-stuffed olives. My version has lots of juicy mushrooms instead, but is still packed with flavour. Serve on a bed of rice, black beans and a big squeeze of zingy lime for flavour-packed, comforting bowls of deliciousness.

TO MAKE THE MUCHROOM ROPA VIEJA

1. In a large pan, add the onion, peppers and olive oil. Cook until soft, around 10–12 minutes.
2. Now add the garlic and mushrooms and cook for 3–5 minutes.
3. Stir in the wine or vinegar and add the paprika, oregano, cumin, soy and cayenne pepper, and stir to combine.
4. Pour in the tomatoes and add the bay leaves. Simmer, stirring occasionally for 10 minutes.
5. Finally add the olives, vinegar and season well.

TO MAKE THE RICE

Add all the ingredients to bowl and mix to combine.

TO SERVE

Serve the ropa vieja over the rice and top with the spring onions.

Difficulty – Medium
Serves – 4
Prep – 15 minutes
Cooking – 40 minutes

1 large organic onion, chopped

2 tbsp olive oil

3 cloves garlic, sliced

1 tsp cumin seeds

1 ½ tbsp smoked paprika

1 tsp dried oregano

1 red peppers, chopped

200g (7oz) tomatoes, sliced

850g (3 ½ cups) veg stock

150g (5.5oz) red lentils, rinsed

2 tbsp sun dried tomato paste

1 tbsp tamari or soy sauce

1 tbsp balsamic vinegar

1 tsp vegan Worcester sauce

1 tsp sea salt

Twist of black pepper

220g (8oz) plant-based mince (ground beef substitute)

200g (7oz) dried pappardelle

Smoky red lentil bolognese with pappardelle

Is there anything more tasty than bolognese loaded onto soft pasta? Originating in 18th-century Italy, it's an absolute classic.

My version uses a combination of lentils and plant-based mince (ground beef substitute) which I think produces a fantastic texture. I used pappardelle here as I love the chunky strips, but you can use your favourite pasta.

TO MAKE THE BOLOGNESE

1. Add the olive oil & onion to a large pan and heat to a medium heat. Fry for about 8–10 minutes until soft and browning.
2. Add in the garlic, spices and stir for another few minutes, then add in the red peppers and fry for 2–3 minutes.
3. Add the lentils along with the tomatoes, stock , balsamic, sun dried tomato and soy sauce.
4. Simmer for 20 minutes, stirring occasionally.
5. In the meantime add the plant-based mince (ground beef substitute) to a pan with a little oil and and fry until coloured.
7. Now add this to the bolognese and mix in well.
8. Season with salt, pepper.

TO SERVE

1. Cook the pasta according to the pack instructions.
2. Top the pasta with the bolognese.

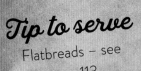

Tip to serve

Flatbreads – see
page 113

INGREDIENTS

Difficulty – Medium
Serves 4
Preparation time : 10 mins
Cooking time : 20 mins

For the curry
1 onion finely chopped
3 tbsp vegetable oil
1 tsp grated ginger
4 cloves garlic sliced
½ tsp cinnamon
10 curry leaves
Pinch of chili flakes
1 tsp ground cumin
1 tsp paprika
1 tsp garam masala
1 tsp sea salt
2 tbsp fresh thyme
400g (14oz) can of
chopped tomatoes
2 cans butter beans
drained

For the coriander chutney
30g (½ cup) fresh
coriander (cilantro)
1 tsp olive oil
1 knob ginger chopped
1 cloves garlic
1 medium red chilli
2 tomatoes chopped
Pinch of sea salt

For the salad;
1 tomato
100g (3.5oz) cucumber
½ red onion
Squeeze lime

Butter bean curry with coriander chutney

This is a simple tomato and butter bean curry is based on the classic Mauritian dish, masala gros pois.

Comforting and wholesome and very easy to make, this is even better when topped with a zingy coriander (cilantro) chutney and a fresh salad.

TO MAKE THE CURRY
1. Add the vegetable oil to a large pan, heat to medium then add the onions, ginger, garlic and spices.
2. Fry for about 8 minutes until soft.
3. Now add the tinned tomatoes and salt and thyme to the pan and simmer for 10 minutes.
4. Turn off the heat and blend until creamy with a stick blender or food processor.
5. Add the butter beans and simmer for 5 more minutes.

TO MAKE THE CHUTNEY
Add all the ingredients to a blender and blend until chunky.

TO MAKE THE SALAD
1. Chop up the tomatoes and cucumber into small cubes.
2. Finely slice the red onion.
3. Add to a bowl and mix to combine.
4. Squeeze the lime over the top.

TO SERVE
Serve the curry with the chutney, salad and flatbreads.

1 large onion, peeled and chopped

2 red or yellow peppers, seeds removed and roughly chopped

4 garlic cloves, peeled

430ml (1 ¾ cups) passata

3 tbsp tomato purée

1 fresh red scotch bonnet chilli, seeds removed (or 1 tsp chilli powder)

2 tbsp fresh rosemary leaves

2 tbsp fresh thyme leaves

1 tbsp smoked paprika

1 tbsp curry powder

30ml (2 tbsp) olive oil

850 ml (3.5 cups) vegetable stock

2 bay leaves

500g (18oz) long-grain rice, rinsed well

300g (10.5oz) frozen peas

Salt and pepper

Handful of of coriander (cilantro) leaves

Jollof rice feast

Jollof rice is a rice dish from West Africa. The dish is typically made with long-grain rice, tomatoes, onions, spices, vegetables and meat in a single pot.

My version has peas which add texture and pops of sweetness. This rice dish is super-comforting and it's great served with a big vegetable curry.

TO MAKE THE JOLLOF RICE

1. Add the onion, passata, tomato purée, chillies, peppers, garlic, rosemary, thyme, curry powder, paprika and olive oil to a food processor and blend until smooth.

2. Transfer to a large pan with a lid and add the mix along with the stock, bay leaves and rice. Stir to combine and bring to the boil.

3. Reduce to a simmer, cover and simmer for 10 minutes, stirring frequently to stop the rice from sticking, until the rice is cooked through. Be careful of the bubbling liquid!

4. Turn off the heat, cover with the lid and leave to steam for 8 minutes without removing the lid.

5. Now add the peas, coriander (cilantro) and season well.

6. Stir well and pop the lid back on for two minutes.

INGREDIENTS

Difficulty – Easy
Prep 10 minutes
Cooking 35 minutes
Serves 4

For the tagine
2 tbsp olive oil
1 onion chopped roughly
1 tsp cumin seeds
1 tsp ground coriander
½ tsp chili flakes
1 tsp cinnamon
½ tsp ground ginger
4 cloves garlic sliced
1 can chopped tomatoes
500ml (2 cups) veg stock
2 tbsp sun dried tomato purée
1 small sweet potato, peeled and cut into chunks
1 red pepper, sliced
½ aubergine (eggplant), sliced
½ courgette (zucchini), sliced
3 carrots, chopped finely
3 tbsp dried apricots, chopped
1 tsp salt and pepper
1 can chickpeas, drained
4 tbsp chopped fresh mint

Toppings
Fresh mint
Runny tahini

300g (10.5oz) cooked rice

Five veg tagine

A fragrant, lightly spiced stew, packed full of flavour and five different vegetables. Add in some chickpeas for some plant-based protein to make a fantastic, healthy and super tasty meal.

TO MAKE THE TAGINE

1. Add the olive oil to a large pan and heat on low/medium then add in the chopped onion.
2. Fry your onion for about 10 minutes until soft and browning.
3. Add in the garlic and spices and stir for a few minutes until fragrant.
4. Add the tomato purée, tomatoes, veg stock, chopped apricots and all the chopped veg. Cover and simmer for about 25 minutes until the veg is soft.
5. Finally add the chickpeas, and salt and pepper to season. Stir in the chopped mint.
6. Serve with the cooked rice, drizzle over the runny tahini and add more fresh mint.

Sticky coconut rice with sesame hoisin mushrooms

This fragrant and tasty meal has its origins in Asia – it's made with beautifully sweet and creamy coconut rice topped with juicy mushrooms and flavoured with toasted sesame, spicy sriracha and rich sweet hoisin. It's a bowl of pure (and slightly spicy) comfort.

TO MAKE THE RICE
1. Add the rice, coconut milk and water to a large saucepan.
2. Simmer on a low heat until the liquid is absorbed, then turn off the heat and pop a lid on the rice for 10 minutes.

TO MAKE THE MUSHROOMS
1. Add the oil and mushrooms to a frying pan and fry on a medium heat for 6–7 minutes until soft, then add in the garlic.
2. Fry for a further minute or so.

TO MAKE THE DRESSING
1. Add the ingredients to a jar and mix to combine.
2. Transfer the dressing to the mushrooms and toss to combine, then heat for 1–2 minutes.

TO SERVE
Spoon the coconut rice into bowls, and top with mushrooms and all the toppings.

INGREDIENTS

Difficultly – Easy
Serves 4
Prep – 10 mnutes
Cooking – 25 minutes

For the rice
200g (7oz) basmati rice, rinsed well
400ml (1 ½ cups) light coconut milk
200ml (¾ cup) water
½ tsp sea salt flakes

For the mushrooms
800g (28oz) mixed mushrooms sliced
3 cloves garlic sliced
2 tbsp olive oil

For the dressing
2 tsp brown rice miso
4 tbsp tamari/soy
2 tbsp rice vinegar
2 tbsp siracha
4 tbsp toasted sesame oil
6 tbsp hoisin sauce

Toppings
2 tbsp crushed roasted peanuts
Handful of coriander (cilantro)
Handful of fresh mint
2 tbsp sesame seeds

INGREDIENTS

Difficulty – Easy
Serves 4
Prep 15 minutes
Cooking 40 minutes

For the pisto stew

3 tbsp olive oil
1 large onion chopped
1 green and yellow pepper, chopped finely
½ tsp chilli flakes
1 tbsp sweet paprika
4 cloves garlic, sliced
1 can tomatoes

For the sautéed veg

2 tbsp olive oil
1 courgette (zucchini) diced
1 aubergine (eggplant) diced
Big pinch of salt
300g (1 ¼ cup) water
1 tsp dried oregano
1 tsp salt & black pepper

For the pa amb tomàquet

½ ciabatta loaf, sliced lengthwise
1–2 garlic cloves peeled
2 ripe tomatoes sliced in half
Extra virgin olive oil
Sea salt flakes

Pisto veg stew with pa amb tomàquet

This delicious veg based dish has all the summery flavours of Spain and it reminds me of sitting in the sun on my balcony in Catalonia.

The pa amb tomàquet is the classic accompaniment and is a Catalan classic. This garlicky toast with fresh tomatoes is fantastic!

TO MAKE THE PISTO

1. Firstly add the oil to a large pan and on a medium heat add the onions, peppers, paprika and chilli flakes.
2. Fry for about 10–12 minutes until soft.
3. Now add the garlic and fry for a further minute.
4. Add the tinned tomatoes. Cover and simmer for 10 minutes.
5. In the meantime, add the aubergine (eggplant), courgette (zucchini) and salt to a separate large frying pan with the olive oil. Fry on medium for 5–6 minutes until soft and crispy on the outside.
6. Transfer the veg to the tomato mix along with the oregano and water, and stir to combine. Cover again and simmer for 10 minutes.
7. Season well with salt and pepper.

TO MAKE THE PA AMB

1. Toast your bread slices.
2. Rub some raw garlic across the top of one side of the toasts.
3. Now squish the tomatoes onto the top of the toasts.
4. Drizzle with olive oil and sprinkle with sea salt.

INGREDIENTS

Difficulty – Medium
Serves 4

For the dough

300g (2 ⅔ cups) self raising white flour

½ tsp sea salt

4 tbsp vegan natural yoghurt

3 tbsp olive oil

100ml (⅓ cup plus 1 tbsp) lukewarm water

For the tomato sauce topping

4 tbsp sun dried tomato paste

1 tsp chipotle paste or ½ tsp chipotle flakes

3 tbsp BBQ sauce

1 tsp smoked paprika

1 tbsp olive oil

Toppings

80g (3oz) sweetcorn, drained

6 cherry tomatoes, sliced in half

1 yellow pepper, chopped

4 mushrooms, sliced

4 tbsp vegan grated cheese – more if you prefer!

For the sauce

3 tbsp mayonnaise or vegan Greek style yoghurt

1 tbsp Bbq sauce

Pinch of sea salt

Squeeze lime juice

2 tbsp water

Smoky chipotle veg pan pizzas

These fun and fluffy pan pizzas are easy to make and have a tex-mex feel, with a tasty BBQ chipotle sauce, lots of veg and a good sprinkling of vegan cheese. These pizzas are extra fun to make in a pan, and it means you can get an extra crisp but fluffy base. They make perfect party food served with some creamy slaw and crispy potatoes.

TO MAKE THE DOUGH

1. Add the dry ingredients to a large bowl, and mix well.
2. Now add the yoghurt, olive oil and water.
3. Mix together with your hands until you create a dough.
4. Tip the dough onto a floured chopping board. Knead for a few minutes until the dough is springy and smooth.

TO MAKE THE PIZZA

1. Form the dough into a ball then divide into four.
2. Roll out each piece of dough onto a floured chopping board.
3. Preheat a frying pan and add a little oil.
4. Place one of the pizza bases into the pan and push to the sides if needed.
5. Now add the tomato topping, veg and plant-based cheese.
6. Cook on medium until the dough fluffs up and becomes a little crispy on the bottom – about 5–6 minutes.
7. Preheat your grill.
8. Transfer the pan to under the grill and cook for 6–7 minutes, until the toppings are cooked and the pizza base sides are a little brown.
9. Repeat with the next pizzas.

TO SERVE

1. Mix the sauce ingredients in a jar.
2. Drizzle or dip the pan pizza in the sauce.

Difficulty – Medium
Serves 4
Prep – 15 minutes
Cooking – 45 minutes

For the pesto

4 tbsp pine nuts, toasted
30g (½ cup fresh) bunch of basil
1 garlic clove
3 tbsp nutritional yeast
½ tsp sea salt
Twist of black pepper
2 tbsp olive oil
Water to loosen

For the pepperonata

3 red, orange or yellow peppers, sliced
1 tbsp olive oil
Pinch of sea salt
1 small onion, chopped into half moons
1 tbsp olive oil
2 garlic cloves

For the dressing

2 tbsp sherry/apple cider vinegar
2 tbsp extra virgin olive oil
1 tbsp maple syrup
Pinch of sea salt
2 tbsp capers

Pesto risotto with pepperonata

Vibrant and green, this risotto sings with lovely Italian flavours. Adding basil pesto to the risotto immediately adds incredible flavour.

The topping of pepperonata – a traditional Italian stew of onions and sweet peppers – adds another layer of texture and flavour. I love the way the juices ooze into the rice. Amazing!

TO MAKE THE PEPPERONATA

1. Heat your oven to 180°C (350°F).
2. Halve and deseed the peppers, then roughly cut into large chunks.
3. Add to a large baking tray and drizzle with olive oil and a sprinkle of salt.
4. Roast the peppers for 25–30 minutes until soft and a little charred.
5. In the meantime, add the onions and olive oil to a saucepan and fry for 7–8 minutes until soft.
6. Add the garlic and fry for a further minute.
7. In a small jar, mix the dressing ingredients and mix to combine.
8. Finally, mix the peppers, onion mix , dressing and capers in a bowl.

TO MAKE THE PESTO

Add all the ingredients to your food processor or high speed blender and whizz until everything is combined to the texture you prefer. You may need to scrape the sides down a few times.

For the risotto

250g (9oz) aborio rice
2 tbsp olive oil
2 onions, chopped roughly
4 cloves garlic, sliced
1.25l (5 ¼ cups) veg stock
3 tbsp nutritional yeast
1 tsp sea salt
Lots of black pepper
4 tbsp of the pesto

Toppings

More pesto to top
Toasted pinenuts
Balsamic syrup/vinegar

TO MAKE THE RISOTTO

1. Add the oil to a large pan on a low to medium heat then add in the chopped onions. Fry for 8–10 minutes until soft. Next add the garlic and fry for a minute, then add rice and stir for a minute . Stir to combine thoroughly.

2. Add the rice and to the pan and stir through to combine.

3. Add 1 ladle of stock at a time until all the liquid is absorbed.

4. Stir in 4 tbsp of the pesto, salt, pepper, and nutritional yeast, and stir to combine.

TO SERVE

Top with the pepperonata, more pesto, toasted pine nuts, and a drizzle of balsamic.

Spring greens spanakopita pie

Difficulty – Medium
Serves 6
Prep – 15 minutes
Cooking – 1 hr

For the greens

1 large leek, cleaned and sliced

1 tbsp olive oil

2 tbsp vegan butter

200g (7oz) green cabbage shredded

4 garlic cloves , crushed

150g (5.5oz) spinach chopped up

20g (⅓ cup) mint, chopped

10g (3 tbsp) dill , chopped

Juice ½ lemon

¼ tsp nutmeg

1 tsp sea salt

200g (7oz) pack firm tofu crumbled

300g (10.5oz) frozen peas

3 tbsp vegan natural yoghurt

270g (10oz) pack vegan filo pastry – 7 sheets

3 tbsp sesame seeds

Spanakopita is a delicious Greek savoury spinach pie. It's a classic, typically made with spinach and cheese and lots of crispy pastry. My version has tons of greens, tofu instead of cheese, and an extra addition of peas to add sweetness. You can eat this warm straight out of the oven, or cold for lunch. Using shop-bought filo makes it very easy to whip up, too!

1. Preheat your oven to 180°C (350°F).
2. In a large pan, add the olive oil and butter, then fry the leek for 7–8 minutes until soft.
3. Just add the shredded cabbage and garlic and fry for 5 minutes.
4. Now add the spinach and herbs and allow to wilt.
5. Crumble the tofu into the mix and add the peas – cook for 2–3 minutes more.
6. Add the yoghurt and nutmeg, and season well.
7. Now compile the pie by filling the filo sheets. Line a large baking tray with parchment paper.
8. Lay out your first filo sheet and spoon some of the mix down the side of the shorter end, in a tube shape.
9. Carefully roll up and over the mixture to create a long tube.
10. Place the first tube onto the prepared baking tray in the middle and curl around to make a little circle.
11. Repeat with the next sheet and then fold it around the first filo tube.
12. Repeat the process with all the sheets and mix to form a wheel shape.
13. Brush with some olive oil and sprinkle with sesame seeds.
14. Bake for 30 minutes until crispy.

Difficulty – Medium
Serves – 6
Prep – 20 minutes
Cooking – 45 minutes

For the bake

2 tbsp olive oil
1 red onion, sliced
4 cloves garlic, sliced
2 red peppers, sliced
1 tbsp smoked paprika
1 can baked beans
1 can black beans, drained
1 tbsp sriracha
1 tbsp soy sauce
Pinch of sea salt
Black pepper

For the cheesy béchamel sauce

2 tbsp vegan butter
2 tbsp plain flour
500ml (2 cups) plant-based milk
3–4 tbsp nutritional yeast
1 tsp garlic powder
Big pinch of sea salt
Twist black pepper

300g (10.5oz) potatoes washed and sliced very thinly
4 tbps vegan grated cheese

Cheesy, bean & potato bake

For me this is classic English comfort food – beans, potatoes and cheese! It's a childhood and family favourite for good reason. The secret ingredient here is... a tin of baked beans! The beans add instant sweetness. The smoked paprika and sriracha bring smoky and chilli heat. This is absolutely delicious when combined with the cheesy sauce and baked in potatoes. So comforting.

TO MAKE THE FILLING

1. Firstly, add the onion to a frying pan along with the oil, and fry on a low heat for 8–10 minutes until soft.
2. Now add the garlic and peppers and fry for 2–3 minutes until soft.
3. Now add all the remaining bake ingredients and simmer for 5 minutes.

TO MAKE THE CHEESY BÉCHAMEL SAUCE

1. Add the butter to a frying pan and melt on a low heat then add the flour. Stir to combine well.
2. Next add the almond milk, and nutritional yeast. Simmer for 5 minutes, stirring constantly to ensure no lumps form. Now season well and remove from the heat.

TO COMPILE

1. Preheat your oven to 180°C (350°F).
2. Slice the potato very thinly.
3. In a medium casserole dish, first add the beans, then add the potatoes layered on top.
4. Now top with cheese sauce and the grated vegan cheese.
5. Bake for 35 minutes until bubbling and the cheese is melted.

PARTY TIME

Spain

Middle East

Vietnam

Mexico

Australia

Wales

China

Difficulty – Medium
Serves 2
Prep – 15 minutes
Cooking – 10 minutes

2 small baguettes

For the pickled veg
1 small carrot, sliced into ribbons with a peeler
½ small cucumber, seeded and sliced into matchsticks
4 tbsp apple cider vinegar
1 tsp maple syrup
Pinch of sea salt

For the Tofu
200g (7oz) firm tofu, sliced into chunky slices
2 tbsp toasted sesame oil
2 tbsp tamari
1 tbsp rice vinegar
Juice of ½ lime
1 tsp maple syrup
1 tbsp garlic granules

1 tbsp oil

For the Peanut sauce
1 tbsp tamari or soy
1 tbsp toasted sesame oil
Juice ½ lime
1 tbsp maple syrup
1 tsp brown rice miso
2 tbsp runny peanut butter
½ tsp chilli flakes

To serve
2 tbsp hoisin sauce
Handful of coriander (cilantro)
Handful of mint

Crispy tofu banh mi with peanut sauce

The first time I ate banh mi in Vietnam, I fell in love. As a sandwich lover, this has everything for me: slightly spicy nutty peanut tofu, tangy quick-picked veg, creamy mango and generous amounts of fresh herbs. All squished into a big fresh baguette.

It's a meal in your hand and pretty filling – but it's so addictive, you'll devour it with no problem at all.

FOR THE PICKLED VEG
1. Slice the veg and add them to a tub. Now add the dressing ingredients and shake to combine.
2. Pop in the fridge until needed.

FOR THE TOFU
1. Add all the tofu dressing ingredients to a large tub, then mix to combine.
2. Now slice the tofu into large slices and transfer to the tub, put the lid on and carefully shake to combine.
3. Allow to marinate for at least 30 minutes – ideally a few hours.
4. In a large pan, heat the oil and fry the tofu for a few minutes each side until brown and crispy, then transfer to a plate.

FOR THE PEANUT SAUCE
Add the ingredients to a large bowl or mason jar and mix well to combine.

TO SERVE
1. Slice the baguette in half lengthwise then layer the hoisin, then tofu, peanut sauce, pickled veg, mint and coriander (cilantro).
2. Spread some more peanut sauce on the other side of the baguette, and press together.

Niki's tip
Tempeh also works
really well here and
adds a different
texture contrast.

For the caramelised onions

2 red onions, cut into strips
2 tbsp olive oil
Pinch of sea salt
2 tbsp vegan Worcester sauce

For the cheesy Béchamel sauce

1 tbsp vegan butter
2 tbsp plain flour
250ml (1 cup) almond milk
3 tbsp nutritional yeast
3 tbsp smoked vegan cheese
Big pinch of sea salt
Twist of black pepper

To top

1 tbsp Worcestershire sauce

4 medium slices fresh sourdough or bread of choice

Rarebit bites with caramelised onions

Have you tried Welsh rarebit? It's the ultimate super tasty cheese on toast. In my version I've added caramelised onions to the cheesy mix, and oh my goodness it's delicious!

I've used smoked vegan cheese here which really enhances the flavour, but you can use non-smoked if you prefer.

TO MAKE THE CARAMELISED ONIONS

1. Cook the onions by adding the oil and sliced onion to a medium pan.
2. Fry on a low heat until soft and caramelised – about 12–15 minutes.
3. Season with salt and pepper.
4. Turn off the heat.

TO MAKE THE CHEESY BÉCHAMEL SAUCE

1. Add the butter to a frying pan and melt on a low heat, then add the flour. Stir to combine well.
2. Next add the almond milk and nutritional yeast.
3. Simmer for 5 minutes, stirring constantly to ensure no lumps form.
4. Now add the cheese and season well.
5. Stir the caramelised onions into the sauce.

TO SERVE

1. Toast the bread, then top each slice with the cheesy mix.
2. Add a little Worcester sauce on top.
3. Pop under the grill for a few minutes until the topping browns a little.

Difficulty – Easy
Makes 4
prep – 10 minutes
cooking – 15 minutes

For the sunflower seed muhamara

190g (7oz) jarred red peppers, drained

2 tbsp olive oil

80g (3oz) sunflower seeds

50g (2oz) stale bread or 3 tbsp breadcrumbs

1 tsp cumin seeds

½ tsp chilli flakes

1 tsp paprika

1 tbsp maple syrup

Juice ½ lemon

1 tsp sea salt

Twist black pepper

For the za'atar yoghurt flatbread

200g (7oz) self raising flour

150g (⅔ cup) plant-based natural yoghurt

Big pinch of sea salt

2 tbsp extra virgin olive oil

Toppings

2 tbsp extra virgin olive oil

4 tbsp Za'atar

Sea salt flakes

Sunflower seed muhamara, with za'atar flatbread

Flatbread is such a classic in middle eastern cuisines. It's perfect for scooping up dips and eating with soups and curries. I've added the zingy and super flavoursome za'atar as a topping here, and it makes the flatbreads taste amazing!

Serve with muhamara, a lightly spiced red pepper dip, and you'll be very happy indeed.

What is Za'atar?

Za'atar is a blend of dried herbs like oregano, marjoram or thyme, and spices like cumin and coriander, with sesame seeds, salt and importantly, sumac, which gives it its delicious tanginess.

TO MAKE THE DIP
Add all the ingredients to a food processor and whizz to a chunky dip.

TO MAKE THE FLATBREADS
1. In a large bowl, add the flour, yoghurt, olive oil and salt.
2. Stir to combine until it comes together, then transfer to a floured board.
3. Knead for a few minutes until you get a springy dough.
4. Heat a large griddle pan or frying pan to medium.
5. Divide the dough into 4, then roll out the first flatbread.
6. Pop it on the griddle pan and allow to cook and char a little on that side then flip to cook to on the other side.
7. Top with olive oil, zaatar and sea salt flakes.
8. Repeat for the rest, then serve the flatbreads with the pepper dip.

INGREDIENTS

Difficulty – Easy
Serves – 4
Prep 10 minutes
Cooking – 1hr

For the potatoes

800g (28oz) potatoes, peeled and cut into small cubes
3 tbsp fresh thyme
2 tbsp olive oil
1 tsp garlic granules
Pinch of sea salt

For the sauce

1 onion, sliced
2 tbsp olive oil
3 cloves garlic, sliced
1 tsp cumin seeds
1 tsp smoked paprika
1 tsp sweet paprika
4 tomatoes, sliced
2 tbsp sun dried tomato paste
Sea salt flakes and black pepper

Garlic sauce

1 tbsp vegan mayo
1 tbsp yoghurt
2 tbsp water
Pinch of salt
½ tsp garlic granules

Toppings

Pinch of dill
Sprig of thyme
Extra virgin olive oil
Balsamic syrup
Chilli flakes

Crispy thyme potatoes with sticky tomatoes

Inspired by my favourite spanish patatas bravas, these crispy delicious roast potatoes are topped with sweet and smokey tomatoes and a creamy garlic sauce. Pure snack heaven!

TO COOK THE POTATOES

1. Preheat your oven to 180°C (350°F).
2. Add the potatoes, olive oil, garlic granules, thyme and a pinch of salt to a large baking tray and place in the oven
3. Roast for about 50 minutes or until crispy on the outside and soft on the inside. Turn occasionally.

TO MAKE THE SAUCE

1. Add the onion and oil to a pan. Fry for 8–10 minutes until caramelised.
2. Now add the garlic and spices and garlic and stir to combine. Fry for a minute or so.
3. Add the tomato paste and tomatoes and simmer for 10 minutes until the tomatoes have broken down.
4. Finally add the salt and pepper.

TO SERVE

Serve the crispy potatoes with the sticky tomatoes, garlic sauce and toppings.

For the sauce

1 tbsp adobo chilli paste
400g (14oz) can chopped tomatoes
1 tsp cumin seeds
1 tsp garlic granules
1 tsp dried oregano
1 tbsp apple cider vinegar
½ tsp sea salt

For the chilaquiles

All of the sauce
80g (3oz) tortilla chips
½ red onion sliced into moons
4 tbsp grated vegan cheese
½ avocado sliced
Handful of fresh coriander (cilantro)
Extra virgin olive oil
Chilli flakes
½ lime juice

Chilaquiles platter

Chilaquiles means 'broken-up old sombrero' and is a popular Mexican brunch dish. It's a taste explosion and makes a brilliant sharing platter.

The tortilla chips are coated in a delicious zingy and smoky tomato sauce, then topped with all the toppings: onion, vegan cheese and avocado. Pop under the grill to crisp it up – amazing! I've cheated a little here and used corn tortilla chips instead of fried stale tortillas.

TO MAKE THE SAUCE

Add the ingredients to a food processor or high speed blender and whizz to smooth.

TO MAKE THE CHILAQUILES

1. Add the sauce to a frying pan and heat on medium for 2–3 minutes.
2. Now add the tortilla chips to the sauce and toss to coat and heat a little.
3. Transfer to a large roasting tin or casserole dish and top with the onion, avocado and cheese.
4. Pop under a heated grill to melt the cheese for 1–2 minutes.
5. Remove and top with fresh coriander (cilantro), olive oil, and chilli flakes.
6. Squeeze lime over the top.
7. Scoop up and eat!

Difficulty – Medium
Serves – aprox 8 burgers
Prep – 10 minutes
Cooking – 25 minutes

For the burgers
1 tbsp olive oil
1 red onion, finely chopped
3 garlic cloves sliced
1 tsp ground cumin
1 tbsp smoked paprika
220g (8 oz) grated fresh beetroot
3 tbsp soy sauce
3 tbsp bbq sauce/ tomato ketchup
2 tbsp balsamic vinegar
Big pinch sea salt and ground black pepper
100g (½ cup) plain flour
1 tsp baking powder
200g (7 oz) firm smoked tofu chopped up very finely

To serve
8 buns of choice
Vegan cheese
Hummus of choice
Tomato chutney
Mayo
Little Gem lettuce leaves

Loaded smoky beetroot burgers

Inspired by beaches and barbecues, my Aussie-style vibrant purple beetroot burgers not only look fun, they taste fantastic! What's the secret? Well, these burgers are made in a slightly different way to standard burgers, as the mix is a little wetter, which means you get a juicier burger. And there's a sneaky secret ingredient too: extra firm smoked tofu, which gives it an amazing texture.

FOR THE BURGERS
1. Add the oil and onion to a frying pan and cook for 6-8 minutes until soft. Now add the garlic and spices, and cook for a further minute.
2. Add the onion mix along with all the ingredients apart from the flour and tofu to a food processor.
3. Whizz until you get a chunky paste.
4. Now transfer to a large bowl along with the flour and tofu. Stir to combine.
5. In a large nonstick frying pan, heat a little oil and spoon a heaped tablespoon of the mixture into the pan. Flatten and spread it out to a round burger shape.
6. Repeat – remember to leave enough room to flip the burgers.
7. Fry for 2-3 minutes on each side until lightly brown.
8. Set aside on a plate.

TO SERVE
Top the buns with Little Gem lettuce, burgers, and toppings of your choice.

Difficulty – Advanced

Serves 4 – makes 8

Prep – 1 hr 30 minutes with dough resting time

Cooking – 30 minutes

For the dough

400g (14oz) plain white flour

¼ tsp sea salt

1 tsp baking powder

7g fast action yeast

1 tsp sugar

2 tbsp olive oil

75ml (⅓ cup) plant-based milk

150ml (⅔ cup) luke warm water

1 tsp rice vinegar

For the sesame fried aubergines

270g (9.5oz) aubergines (eggplant), sliced into thin circles

2 tbsp toasted sesame oil

Pinch of sea salt flakes

For the Mayo

8tbsp vegan mayo

1 tbsp gochujang

For the peanut salad

½ cucumber, sliced

1 large carrot, peeled and julienned

4 spring onion, sliced finely

Big handful of fresh coriander and mint

4 tbsp toasted, salted and crushed peanuts

2 tbsp soy sauce

2 tbsp toasted sesame oil

Bao buns with sesame, aubergine & peanut salad

I'm obsessed with bao buns – the soft and pillowy steamed texture is amazing! The gua bao originated from the coastal regions of Fujian province in China, and their popularity has spread over the world for good reason. The filling is important as well. You need a combination of creamy and crispy to contrast with the softness of the buns.

The crunchy peanut salad here is fantastic, combined with the creamy and slightly spicy mayo and crispy fried aubergine.

TO MAKE THE DOUGH

1. Add the flour, salt and baking powder to a large bowl and mix well.
2. In small bowl, mix the yeast, sugar, olive oil and leave for a minute or so.
3. Create a hole in the middle of the flour and gradually add the milk, water, yeast mix and rice vinegar and mix until you have a dough.
4. Tip the dough onto a floured chopping board. Knead for a few minutes until the dough is springy. Add more flour if needed.
5. Transfer back to the bowl and cover with a damp cloth for about an hour. The dough should have doubled in size.
6. Transfer back onto the floured chopping board and knead again to knock back.
7. Now form into a ball and divide into 8 equal parts.
8. In the palm of your hand, roll each piece of dough into a ball.
9. Use a rolling pin to roll out each ball, one by one, into an oval shape about 3–4mm thick.
10. Rub the surface of the ovals with oil and brush a little oil over a skewer. Place a skewer in the centre of each oval. Fold the dough over a skewer, then slowly pull out.
11. Place each bao onto a board lined with baking paper.
12. Brush them with a little oil.

13. Leave to prove in a warm place for 1 hour, or until doubled in size.

14. Use a steamer to steam the buns for 8 minutes until puffed up (you'll need to do this in batches).

TO MAKE THE SALAD

1. Chop the veg finely and add to a bowl with the peanuts, herbs, soy sauce and sesame oil.

2. Mix to combine.

TO COOK THE AUBERGINE

1. Add half the sesame oil to a frying pan, then add half the aubergine (eggplant) and a pinch of of salt.

2. Fry for a few minutes on each side until crispy.

3. Repeat with the remaining aubergine (eggplant).

TO MAKE THE MAYO

Mix the mayo and gochujang in a bowl.

TO SERVE

Prise open each bun and fill with the mayo, crispy aubergine (eggplant) and salad.

Other filling options

- Delicious with katsu tofu (page 77)
- Add satay peanut sauce (page 61)
- No gochujang? Use sriracha instead
- Swap the aubergine for mushrooms or peppers

SNACKS

India

Japan

Canada

China

Jamaica

Korea

Denmark

Europe

Italy

Difficulty – Easy
Serves 2
Prep – 10 minutes
Cooking – 5 minutes

**Chunky sun dried
tomato dip**
150g (5.5oz) sun blush/
sun dried tomatoes
20g (⅓ cup) fresh basil
60g (2oz) cherry
tomatoes
1 clove garlic
5 tbsp nutritional yeast
3 tbsp extra virgin olive oil
Big pinch sea salt
Pinch black pepper
Pinch chilli flakes

4 slices chunky bread
toasted

Toppings
2–4 tbsp vegan cream
cheese
Cherry tomatoes/
heritage tomatoes, sliced
Handful olives sliced
Drizzle extra virgin olive oil
Dill or basil

Sundried tomato & cream cheese bruschetta

I could imagine sitting in the mediterranean sun, eating this gorgeous and flavour popping bruschetta. They're layered with creamy vegan cream cheese, topped with an amazing sundried tomato dip, and finished off with fresh tomatoes, olives and herbs.

TO MAKE THE BRUSCHETTA
1. First a layer of creamy vegan cream cheese,
2. Top with an amazing sun dried tomato dip
3. Add more fresh tomatoes, olives and fresh herbs to finish.
3. Toast the bread, then top with the dip.

TO MAKE THE DIP
Add all the ingredients to a food processor and blitz to a chunky dip.

Tip to serve
You can eat these gorgeous toasts for breakfast, lunch or a snack and the dip makes a brilliant sandwich filler!

INGREDIENTS

Difficulty – Medium
2–4 servings
Prep – 10 minutes
Cooking – 15 minutes

For the pancakes
150g (1 ¼ cups) plain white flour
Pinch of sea salt
120ml (½ cup) boiling water

For the dipping sauce
3 tbsp tamari
1 tbsp rice wine
2 tbsp toasted sesame oil
½ tsp chilli flakes
2 tbsp maple syrup
Juice ½ lime
2 tbsp sesame seeds
1 clove garlic minced
1 thumb ginger grated

For the filling
1 tbsp coconut oil melted
1.5 tbsp toasted sesame oil
1.5 tbsp plain flour
2 tsp Chinese five spice powder
½ tsp salt, or to taste

3 spring onions sliced

Scallion pancakes (Cong You Bing)

I think you're going to love these these fluffy, crispy and incredibly flavoursome little Chinese pancake breads! Layered with toasted sesame oil, five spice and spring onions, they become crispy and flaky with the layers in the bread. Dip in the delicious dipping sauce for a taste explosion.

TO MAKE THE PANCAKES
1. Add the flour and salt to a large bowl and mix to combine.
2. Add the boiling water and mix well.
3. Transfer the dough to a well floured surface and knead for 2–3 minutes until smooth.
4. Form a ball, then coat it with oil and pop back in the bowl and cover the bowl with damp cloth. Leave for 30 min.

TO MAKE THE FILLING
1. In a jar, mix the flour, five spice, salt, melted coconut oil and toasted sesame oil.
2. Finely chop the spring onions.

TO MAKE THE DIPPING SAUCE
Add all the ingredients to a jar and mix thoroughly.

TO MAKE THE PANCAKES
1. Dust a surface with flour then add the dough and knead the dough again. Then roll it out with a rolling pin into a thin rectangle shape
2. Brush the filling mixture onto the dough to the edges.
3. Roll into a rope shape, and then cut into 6 even cylinders.
4. Dust with the surface with flour again.
5. Stand each piece on its end, flatten with your hand, then then roll it flat into a circle.
6. Heat a frying pan to medium, then place a pancake in to cook.
7. Cook for a couple of minutes, then flip over when golden brown on the bottom. Cook on the other side. Repeat.

TO SERVE
Serve the pancakes dipped into the dipping oil.

4 apples of choice
Lolly sticks

For the caramel layer
4 medjool dates, pitted
100ml (⅓ cup plus 1 tbsp) oat milk
Pinch sea salt
2 tbsp peanut butter

For the chocolate
100g (3.5oz) dark dairy-free chocolate
1 tbsp coconut oil

Toppings
Choc chips
Chopped nuts – pistachios, salted peanuts
Desiccated coconut
Crushed cookies
Sea salt flakes
Seeds

Caramel choc apples

A fun take on the toffee apple – these cute little apples on sticks are easy to make and so delicious!

The apple slices are topped with a sticky layer of date caramel, then topped with chocolate and fun toppings of your choice – I love crushed pistachio and salted peanuts.

TO MAKE THE DATE CARAMEL
Add all the ingredients to a food processor and blend to a smooth paste.

TO MAKE THE APPLE STICKS
1. Melt the chocolate and coconut oil in in the microwave in a glass bowl, on a low heat in 10 second increments until it's melted.
2. Line a large baking tray with baking paper.
3. Slice the apples into 1 cm slices, then insert a stick into the base of each slice.
4. Spread one tablespoon of the caramel over the top of one side then dip the slices into the melted chocolate to cover both sides.
5. Place on the baking tray and sprinkle with toppings of your choice.
6. Place in the fridge to firm up and set.

Peanut drops

These nutty sweet Jamaican snacks are totally moreish. You can use roasted salted peanuts for that sweet salty taste, or roasted unsalted to make them sweet and nutty. Peanut drops make a perfect high protein snack, and they taste incredible.

INGREDIENTS

Difficulty – Easy
Makes 9–10
Prep – 5 minutes
Cooking – 15 minutes

200g (7oz) roasted peanuts – natural or salted
60ml (¼ cup) maple syrup
3 tbsp peanut butter
2 tbsp grated ginger or 1 tsp ground ginger
1 tsp vanilla extract

TO MAKE THE PEANUT DROPS

1. Add the maple syrup, peanut butter, ginger and vanilla extract to a jar.
2. Mix well until smooth.
3. Add the peanuts and sauce to a large bowl and mix to combine thoroughly.
4. Preheat your oven to 150°C (300°F).
5. Line a baking tray then scoop up heaped teaspoons of the mix and place onto the baking tray.
6. Press down a bit.
7. Bake the peanut drops for 15 minutes until they're golden brown.
8. Remove from the oven and allow to cool.

Difficulty – Easy
Serves 4 as a snack
Prep – 5 minutes
Cooking – 10 minutes

1 tbsp oil
3 spring onions, sliced
3 cloves garlic, sliced
1 tbsp fresh ginger, minced

300g (10.5oz) edamame beans
2 tbsp light soy sauce or tamari
2 tbsp sweet chilli sauce
2 tsp toasted sesame oil
½ tsp chilli flakes

3 tbsp toasted sesame seeds

Sweet chilli edamame

A quick and incredibly tasty snack, full of zingy asian flavours like sweet chilli, ginger, soy and toasted sesame. They are totally addictive – be warned!

TO MAKE THE SWEET CHILI EDAMAME

1. Add the oil to a pan, heat to medium, then add the spring onion. Fry for 4–5 minutes then add the garlic and ginger.
2. Cook until fragrant – around 30 to 60 seconds.
3. Now add in the edamame, soy, sweet chilli, toasted sesame and a pinch of chilli flakes.
4. Heat for 2–3 minutes.

TO SERVE

Serve topped with toasted sesame seeds.

Bhel puri

INGREDIENTS

Difficulty – Easy
Serves 4–6
Prep – 10 minutes
Cooking – 20 minutes

For the bhel puri
50g (1.5oz) puffed rice
60g (3oz) Bombay mix
200g (7oz) cooked potatoes chopped into tiny cubes
½ red onion, finely chopped
2 tomato, finely chopped
3 tbsp roasted and salted peanuts
20g (¼ cup) coriander (cilantro), finely chopped
20g (⅓ cup) mint, roughly chopped
¼ green chili, finely chopped
1 tsp chaat masala (spice mix)
Pinch of sea salt flakes

For the dressing
Mix 2 tbsp tamarind chutney with the juice of 1 lime

4 poppadoms to serve

Bhel puri is a popular savoury snack originating in India. It's a type of chaat – the roadside snacks from stalls or food carts across South Asia in India, Pakistan, Nepal and Bangladesh.

This super tasty and crunchy snack is made from puffed rice, vegetables and a tangy tamarind sauce. I serve it in crispy popadoms, and it makes the perfect sharing or party food. Make sure you eat it straight away while it's crispy though!

TO MAKE THE BHEL PURI
1. Mix all the ingredients in a large bowl and toss to combine.
2. Mix the tamarind chutney and lime in a jar.
3. Cook the popadoms according to the pack instructions.
4. Serve the bhel puri in the popadoms.
5. Serve and eat immediately.

Difficulty – Medium
Makes 10–12
Prep – 15 minutes
Cooking – 40 minutes

For the balsamic onions

2 large red onions
2 tbsp olive oil
3 cloves garlic
2 tbsp balsamic vinegar
Big pinch of sea salt

For the fritters

120g (1 cup) plain flour
1 tsp baking powder
4 tbsp nutritional yeast
1 tsp salt
2 sprigs of fresh thyme
275ml (1 ⅛ cups) water
200g (7oz) cooked spaghetti
1 tbsp olive oil

4 tbsp vegetable oil

For the sauce

1 red onion sliced
2 tbsp olive oil
2 cloves garlic sliced
1 tsp smoked paprika
1 tsp sweet paprika
1 tsp dried oregano
4 tomatoes sliced
2 tbsp tomato paste
50ml (¼ cup) water
Sea salt flakes and black pepper

Toppings

Fresh herbs – dill, thyme

Spaghetti fritters with sticky tomatoes

Use up your leftover spaghetti with this fun Italian dish – frittelle di spaghetti. It's traditionally made with eggs, herbs and cheese but my version has the addition of caramelised balsamic tomatoes, lots of thyme and a sticky tomato mix topping. I think you'll love them – they're squidgy on the inside and crispy on the outside. Fun, thrifty and delicious!

TO MAKE THE ONIONS

1. Firstly peel and slice the onions into thin rings.
2. Add them along with the oil to a pan and fry for about 10 minutes until very soft.
3. Now add the garlic and fry for a further minute.
4. You can now add the balsamic and salt. Stir to combine.

TO MAKE THE FRITTERS

1. In a large bowl, add all dry ingredients then add the water.
2. Stir to form a thick batter.
3. Now add the cooked onions and spaghetti and mix very well to coat.
4. Allow to sit for 15 minutes.
5. Heat the vegetable oil in a large nonstick frying pan so there is a shallow layer of oil.
6. Spoon 2 tbsp of the mix into the pan, then press down.
7. Fry for 4–5 minutes on this side until crispy and golden. Flip and repeat with the rest of the mix.

TO MAKE THE SAUCE

1. In the meantime, add the onion and oil to a pan. Fry for 8–10 minutes until caramelised.
2. Now add the garlic and spices and garlic and stir to combine. Fry for a minute or so.
3. Add the tomato paste, tomatoes and water, and simmer for 10 minutes until the tomato has broken down.
4. Finally add the salt, pepper.
5. Serve the crispy fritters with the sticky tomato and toppings.

Difficulty – Easy
Prep – 5 minutes
Cooking – 5 minutes

For the popcorn
50g (1.5oz) dried corn kernels
1 tbsp oil

Toppings
3 tbsp melted vegan butter
1 tbsp maple syrup
1 tbsp smoked paprika
½ tsp ground cumin
½ sea salt
2 tbsp nutritional yeast

Smoky maple popcorn

There's something magical about watching those corn kernels transform into fluffy popcorn with such riotous abandon in the pan. Sweet toppings are great, but why not try something different? The smoky, cheesy, buttery mix here is totally addictive!

TO MAKE THE POPCORN
1. Using a large pan with a lid, heat to a high heat and add the oil.
2. Now throw in a few pieces of corn and cover. Wait until they pop and expand into popcorn.
3. Now add the rest of the corn and replace the lid.
4. The corn will start popping, and soon it will all pop.
5. Turn off the heat and set aside.

TO MAKE THE TOPPING
1. Melt the butter, then add to the popcorn in the pan along with the maple syrup.
2. Now mix the remaining dry ingredients in a jar then sprinkle over.
3. Toss the popcorn to coat well.

200g (7oz) firm tofu drained

For the sauce
2 tsp brown rice miso
3 tbsp gochujang paste
3 tbsp toasted sesame oil
2 tbsp soy sauce
1 tsp garlic powder
2 tbsp maple syrup
1 tsp ground ginger
2 tbsp rice vinegar

Dipping sauce
All the remaining sauce
2 tbsp toasted sesame oil
2 tsp soy sauce

Toppings
Sesame seeds

Sticky miso tofu with dipping sauce

These crispy spicy Korean-inspired tofu bites pack a flavour punch! Sweet and spicy at the same time, they have an amazing texture: crispy on the outside and soft on the inside.

The leftover dressing makes the most wonderful dipping sauce, with toasted sesame oil and soy sauce added.

TO MAKE THE MISO TOFU
1. To make super crispy tofu, I recommend pressing the tofu to remove as much moisture as possible.
2. Now make the dressing by adding all the ingredients to a jar. Mix to combine.
3. Dry the tofu and then cut in half down the middle lengthwise. Now cut each slice into 4 triangles, making 8 in total.
4. Pour the dressing into a large tub, then coat each slice in the dressing and pop in the tub.
5. Cover and transfer to the fridge for a couple of hours to marinate.

TO COOK
1. Add a little oil to a preheated griddle or frying pan and add the tofu in batches.
2. Allow to cook on each side for a few minutes until crispy and a little charred on each side.
3. Repeat.
4. Transfer the excess dressing to a jar. Mix in the toasted sesame oil and soy sauce.

TO SERVE
Sprinkle some sesame seeds on top, then dip in the dressing.

INGREDIENTS

Difficulty – Advanced
Makes – approx 30
Prep – 10 minutes
Cooking – 20 minutes

Dry ingredients

150g (1 ¼ cups) self-raising flour
1 tsp baking powder
1 tsp baking soda
Pinch of salt
40g (¼ cup) caster sugar

Wet ingredients

250g (1 cup) plant-based milk
1 tsp vanilla extract
2 tbsp veg oil of choice
1 tsp apple cider vinegar
1 ripe banana, mashed
1 flax egg (1 tbsp of ground flax seeds + 2 tbsp of water mixed, set aside for 10 minutes)

Oil for frying

Optional fillings

Cherry jam
Choc chips

Banana and jam aebleskiver

Æbleskiver are Danish snacks made in spherical shapes. The name actually means "apple slices". although apples are not usually an ingredient! These delicious little snacks are like a cross between mini pancakes, yorkshire puddings and donuts – very yum.

I use an aebleskiver pan to make them into little balls, but you can just use a frying pan and create them like mini pancakes.

TO MAKE THE ÆBLESKIVER

1. Mix the dry ingredients in a large bowl.
2. Add all the wet ingredients and mix to combine well.
3. Now heat your aebleskiver pan to medium heat and add a tiny bit of oil into each round hole.
4. Spoon a little batter in the rounds until almost filled, then add your filling (just ¼ tsp of jam or 2 choc chips).
5. Spoon a little more batter over the top then when the edges are becoming solid and the batter is bubbling, you can flip them over with a teaspoon.
6. They are ready when both sides are puffy and golden brown.
7. Repeat with all the mix.
8. Serve with a dusting of icing sugar.

IF YOU DON'T HAVE AN ÆBLESKIVER PAN

1. Spoon one tablespoon of the mixture and spread it out to form a small round pancake shape.
2. Immediately add ¼ tsp of the jam to the middle.
3. Now spoon a little more of the pancake mix on to the top to cover.
4. Fry for 1–2 minutes until the underside is firm, you should see little bubbles forming on top.
5. Carefully flip the pancakes and then cook for another minute or so until the pancakes are cooked through and slightly golden.
6. Repeat with all the mixture and fruit, and set aside on a plate.

SWEET TREATS

Australia

South America

Asia

Mexico

USA

Netherlands

France

Germany

South Africa

Europe

Difficulty – Easy
Makes about 20
Prep – 15 minutes

For the chocolate orange truffles
200g (7oz) dairy-free dark chocolate, broken up
100ml (⅓ cup plus 1 tbsp) plant-based milk
2 tbsp maple syrup
1 tsp vanilla extract
1 tsp orange extract

Toppings
2 tbsp cocoa powder

For the chocolate coating
50g (2oz) dairy-free dark chocolate, broken up
1 tsp coconut oil
Pistachios, crushed

Choc orange truffles

Chocolate orange truffles are absolutely delicious and you'll be surprised how easy they are to make.

Smooth, creamy and decadent, you can keep it simple and roll them in cacao, or for extra deliciousness, coat them in a layer of chocolate! In this recipe I half-coat them. Make them for your friends to put a smile on their face.

TO MAKE THE CHOCOLATE ORANGE TRUFFLES
1. Add the chocolate to a glass bowl.
2. Pour the milk and maple syrup into a small saucepan, then bring to the boil briefly over a medium heat, stirring occasionally.
3. Now stir in the vanilla & orange extract.
4. Now pour over the chocolate, leave to sit for a minute, then stir until the chocolate has melted and the mix is smooth and glossy.
5. Chill in the fridge for a few hours until set.
6. Using a teaspoon, scoop out the mixture and roll to form into balls using your hands.
7. Add the cocoa powder to a bowl then roll the truffles until coated.

TO COAT IN CHOCOLATE
1. Add the the chocolate and coconut oil to a glass bowl and heat in a microwave on low, in 10 second increments until melted.
2. Dip the half the truffles into melted chocolate and sprinkle with crushed pistachios.
3. Add to a tray and pop in the fridge to firm up.
4. Store in the fridge.

INGREDIENTS

Difficulty – Easy
Prep – 10 minutes
Cooking – 35 minutes

For the pine tart
290g (10oz) pineapple rings in juice (drained weight)
5 tbsp of the pineapple juice
5 tbsp brown sugar
2 tsp ground ginger
3 tbsp vegan butter
1 tsp vanilla extract
1 sheet vegan puff pastry
5 tbsp orange marmalade

For the creamy yoghurt
6 tbsp vegan greek style yoghurt
1 tbsp maple syrup
1 tsp vanilla extract

Pine tart

This fun and very easy to make pine tart is inspired by cute little guyanese pine tarts.

My version couldn't be easier to make, as it's made from store cupboard ingredients with a few extras to make it special. It's puff pastry topped with marmalade for a zingy contrast to the super sweet pineapple, drizzled with a sweet and gingery sugar syrup, then baked until crispy on the outside and gooey on the inside.

TO MAKE THE PINE TART

1. Add the sugar, ginger, butter and pineapple juice to a saucepan.
2. Cook, stirring occasionally, for 2–3 minutes or until syrupy.
3. Set aside to cool slightly.
4. Preheat oven to 180°C (350°F).
5. In a medium rectangular casserole dish, grease with a little oil then place the puff pasty over the top. Press down and up the sides.
6. Now spoon the marmalade over the base of the pastry and spread over and into the edges.
7. Place the pineapple rings on top, then spoon over the syrup.
8. Pleat and fold in the edges of the puff pastry around the tart.
9. Bake for 30 minutes or until the pastry is golden.

TO MAKE THE YOGHURT
Mix all the ingredients in a small bowl.

TO SERVE
Top the tart with the yoghurt.

For the crumble layer

4 tbsp ground almonds
4 tbsp oats of choice
2 tbsp desiccated coconut
2 tbsp sunflower seeds
2 tbsp almond butter
2 tbsp maple syrup

For the miso caramel

3 tbsp maple syrup
1 tsp white miso
6 tbsp coconut milk
1 tbsp coconut oil
Pinch sea salt
1 tsp vanilla

For the matcha mix

6 tbsp coconut or vegan
greek style yoghurt
1 tsp matcha
2 tbsp maple syrup
1 tsp vanilla powder or
extract

Matcha pots with miso caramel

This dessert is easy and delicious, with some unique Asian flavours. Green matcha is swirled into the creamy coconut yoghurt layer, an incredible miso caramel layer, and then crispy, crumbly granola with coconut.

The crumble makes a lovely granola – so why not double the batch, and eat it with milk for breakfast!

TO MAKE THE CRUMBLE

1. Preheat the oven to 180°C (350°F).
2. In a bowl, mix the crumble mix together so everything is combined, then transfer to a baking tray.
3. Bake for 12–15 minutes until lightly toasted. Set aside.

TO MAKE THE MISO CARAMEL

1. Heat the ingredients in a saucepan on a low heat. Stir constantly while it's bubbling for 8–10 minutes to thicken.
2. Turn off the heat, add the vanilla and stir to combine.
3. Set aside.

TO MAKE THE MATCHA MIX

Mix all the ingredients in a small bowl.

TO COMPILE

Layer the crumble, then the yoghurt mix into two medium or four small pots. Next add some caramel and yoghurt. Repeat.

Niki's tip
Serve with a dollop of vegan ice cream!

Flourless mince pie brownies

Mince pie brownies are a joyous combination of flavours. They are gooey, moist, fruity, richly chocolatey and totally addictive!

These grain-free brownies have added homemade or shop-bought vegan mincemeat – whichever you prefer. Brilliant for the festive period... or any time of year.

INGREDIENTS

8–10 servings
Difficulty – Easy
Prep – 15 minutes
Cooking – 20 minutes

Wet ingredients

200ml (¾ cup) plant-based milk

100g (3.5oz) vegan dark chocolate

3 tbsp peanut or almond butter

2 tsp. vanilla extract

1 tsp almond extract

Dry ingredients

70g (¼ cup packed) light brown sugar

100g (3.5oz) ground almonds

40g (⅓ cup) raw cacao powder

1 tsp baking powder

½ tsp bicarbonate of soda (baking soda)

Pinch of sea salt flakes

1 tsp all spice

175g (6.5oz) vegan mincemeat

4 tbsp dark chocolate chips, plus more choc chips to top

TO MAKE THE BROWNIES

1. Heat the oven to 180°C (350°F).
2. Line the base and sides of a medium baking tray with baking paper
3. Add the wet ingredients to a saucepan and gently heat. Stir gently with a whisk to combine.
4. Now add all the dry ingredients to a large bowl, and mix to combine.
5. Transfer the wet mix into the bowl, and fold in to combine. Now stir in the mincemeat and choc chips.
6. Spoon everything into the baking tray. Press into the sides.
7. Sprinkle the additional choc chips over the top.
8. Bake for 20 minutes, then remove from the oven and allow to cool and set for at least an hour.
9. Slice and store in an airtight container for up to 4 days.

Difficulty – Medium
Makes 16
Prep – 15 minutes
Cooking – 20 minutes

For the cake
300ml (1 ¼ cups) coconut milk drink
80g (⅓ cup) vegetable oil
1 tbsp cider vinegar
1 tsp vanilla extract
250g (2 cups) self-raising flour
50g (2oz) desiccated coconut
150g (¾ cup) caster sugar
Zest of 2 lemons
1 tsp baking powder

For the filling
4 tbsp ginger jam

For the chocolate
300g (10oz) dark chocolate
2 tbsp coconut oil

Topping
100g (3.5oz) desiccated coconut

Coconut ginger lamingtons

This is my version of a the iconic Australian dessert – the Lamington. It's a light and fluffy coconut sponge with a ginger jam filling, dipped in rich dark chocolate and desiccated coconut.

I think the flavour combination is fantastic – tropical, light and indulgent at the same time. Ginger, coconut and chocolate is a dreamy match made in heaven.

Store them in the fridge and only take out when you want to eat them, to ensure the chocolate is cold and crispy.

TO MAKE THE CAKE
1. Preheat the oven to 180°C (350°F).
2. In a bowl, stir in the coconut milk, cider vinegar and vanilla.
3. In a separate bowl, add the flour, sugar, baking powder, coconut, and lemon zest. Stir to combine.
4. Now add in the liquid to the dry mix. Stir thoroughly to combine.
5. Pour the mixture into a lined large rectangular baking tray, and place into the oven to bake for about 20 minutes or until cooked through.
6. Once baked, remove from the oven and allow to cool.
7. When cool, cut the cake into 32 squares, top half with the ginger jam, then sandwich back together.

TO MAKE THE COATING
1. Melt the chocolate and coconut oil together in a bain-marie (a bowl suspended just above boiling water in a pan.)
2. Add the desiccated coconut to a large bowl.
3. Balance the cake on a fork and dip into the melted chocolate.
4. Sprinkle the coconut over the chocolate then place on a baking tray
5. Repeat.
6. Pop in the fridge to set.

INGREDIENTS

Difficulty – Easy
Makes 12
Prep – 10 minutes
Cooking – 20 minutes

Dry mix
150 (1 ¼ cups) self-raising flour
75g (2.5oz) ground almonds
2 tsp baking powder
2 tsp cinnamon
120g (⅔ cup) caster sugar

Wet mix
1 tsp vanilla extract
200ml (¾ cup) almond milk
75ml (¼ cup) vegetable oil
1 tsp apple cider vinegar

2 large ripe bananas, peeled and mashed
2 tbsp Biscoff paste

For the caramel centre
4 medjool dates, pitted
100ml (⅓ cup plus 1 tbsp) oat milk
Pinch of sea salt
2 tbsp peanut butter

Banoffee Biscoff muffins

My friends and family love these cute and deliciously decadent little muffins!

Fluffy banana and Biscoff (a match made in heaven) muffins with a centre of gooey date caramel. Need I say more?

They also work really well without the caramel centre if preferred.

TO MAKE THE CUPCAKES
1. Preheat the oven to 180°C (350°F).
2. Line a muffin tray with 12 cases.
3. Mix the dry ingredients in a large bowl.
4. Mix the almond milk, vanilla, vegetable oil an cider vinegar in a jug then pour into the dry mix. Stir until smooth.
5. Add the banana and Biscoff and mix well.
6. Divide the mixture equally between the 12 muffin cases and bake for 20 minutes.
7. To check they're baked, insert a skewer into the middle of the cupcakes – if it comes out clean, they're done.
8. Leave to cool, then cut small holes in the centre of the cupcakes. You can use a small sharp knife to hollow out the centres.

TO FILL
1. Add all the caramel ingredients to a food processor and blitz.
2. Spoon the mixture in to each of the muffin holes.

For the base

180g (6.5oz) walnuts
80g (3oz) gingernut biscuits
1 tsp ground ginger
6 medjool dates, pitted
2 tbsp cacao powder
4 tbsp ground almonds
4 tbsp vegan butter, melted
Pinch of sea salt

For the filling

140g (5oz) vegan cream cheese
250g (1 cup) sweetened condensed coconut milk or 200g (¾ cup) coconut cream with 50ml (3 tbsp) maple syrup)
3 tbsp cacao powder
1 tsp vanilla extract
Pinch of chilli flakes
Pinch of sea salt
½ tsp cinnamon
½ tsp ground ginger

100g (3.5oz) dairy-free dark chocolate
2 tbsp coconut oil

Toppings

Choc chips
Fruit of choice

Creamy chocolate chilli cheesecake

The flavours of this lightly spiced and super creamy chocolate cheesecake combine the Mexican classics of chilli, cinnamon and chocolate – it's a subtle but heady mix. This is a pretty special cheesecake! And for the base, I sneaked in gingernut biscuits and it's incredible – no cooking required!

TO MAKE THE BASE

1. Blend the walnuts and gingernuts in a food processor to a chunky crumb.
2. Now add all the remaining ingredients to a food processor and blitz to combine.
3. Grease and line a loose bottomed cake tin with baking paper, then press the base mix on to the bottom and up the sides.

TO MAKE THE CHOC FILLING

1. Add the cream cheese, coconut, cacao, vanilla, spices and salt to a food processor and whizz until you get a super smooth paste. You may need to scrape down the sides a few times.
2. Break up the chocolate and add it. and the coconut oil, to a saucepan. Heat very gently on a low heat until melted. Don't overstir.
3. Now add it to the mix in the food processor and blend until very smooth.
4. Spoon on to the base, then chill in the fridge for at least an hour or until it's set.

Ginger malva pudding

Malva pudding is an amazing sweet pudding of South African origin. It's very like sticky toffee pudding, but contains apricot jam and has a spongy caramelised texture – its quite special and totally addictive. The gorgeous caramel sauce is poured over the warm cake and makes it sticky and gooey.

INGREDIENTS

Difficulty – Easy
12 slices
Prep – 5 minutes
Cooking – 25 minutes

Dry ingredients
250g (2 cups) plain flour
200g (1 cup packed) light brown sugar
2 tsp baking powder
1 tsp baking soda
3 tsp ground ginger
Pinch of salt

Wet ingredients
1 tbsp apple cider vinegar
125ml (½ cup) plant-based milk
5 tbsp apricot jam
50ml (¼ cup) veg oil

For the sauce
80g (6 tbsp) vegan butter
80g (⅓ cup packed) light brown sugar
250g (1 cup) coconut cream
1 tsp vanilla extract

TO MAKE THE PUDDING

1. Preheat the oven to 180°C (350°F).
2. Line a small baking tray with baking paper.
3. Add the dry ingredients to a mixing bowl and mix together.
4. In a small jug, add the vinegar to the plant-based milk and let it curdle.
5. You can now add this along with the apricot jam and oil to the dry mix, and mix well to form a batter.
6. Transfer the batter to your baking tray and smooth to the edges.
7. Bake for 25 minutes or until a toothpick inserted into the centre of the cake comes out clean.

TO MAKE THE SAUCE

1. When the cake is almost finished cooking, start making your sauce.
2. Add the butter to a saucepan and allow to melt. Add the sugar and coconut cream and heat together until it reaches a simmer, stirring continusly.
3. Remove from the heat and add the vanilla extract.
4. When the cake comes out the oven, poke holes all over it with a toothpick and then pour the sauce over, making sure it'ss distributed evenly across the whole pudding.
5. Allow the sauce to sink in, and then cut into squares.
6. If you have extra sauce, drizzle over the top.

Difficulty – Easy
Makes about 12
Prep – 10 minutes
Cooking – 10 minutes

130g (9 tbsp (1 stick + 1 tbsp) vegan butter
175g (¾ cup packed) light brown sugar
1 tsp vanilla extract
180g (2 cups) rye flour
½ tsp xanthan gum
Pinch of sea salt
1 tsp baking powder
1 tsp bicarbonate of soda
5 tbsp cacao powder
75ml (¼ cup) oat milk
100g (3.5oz) dairy-free dark chocolate chips
100g (3.5oz) glacé cherries, sliced in half

Chocolate cherry rye cookies

These American style large and fluffy cookies are amazing! They're soft, squidgy and brownie-like. The pop of sweet cherries make them even better.

Make sure you allow them to cool before eating – if you can!

TO MAKE THE COOKIES
1. Preheat your oven to 180°C (350°F).
2. Add the butter, sugar and vanilla extract to a bowl and mix to combine thoroughly.
3. In a separate large bowl, mix the dry ingredients then add in the butter mix and oat milk.
4. Mix until you get a sticky dough.
5. Now add the choc chips and mix in to combine.
6. Line a large baking tray with baking paper.
7. Flour a chopping board, then roll out the dough.
8. Cut out round cookies with a cookie cutter or glass then add to the baking tray – make sure they aren't too crowded.
9. Top the cookies with the cherry halves.
10. Bake for about 10 minutes, until set but not hard.
11. Allow to cool before eating.

INGREDIENTS

Difficulty – Easy
Serves about 8
Prep – 10 minutes
Cooking – 40 minutes

Dry mix
150g (1 ⅓ cups) self-raising flour
100g (3.5oz) ground almonds
1 tsp baking powder
½ tsp bicarbonate of soda
70g (⅔ cup) cocoa powder
260g (1 ¼ cups packed) light brown sugar
Pinch of sea salt

Wet mix
1 tsp vanilla extract
250ml (1 cup) warm water
75ml (¼ cup) oat milk
100g (½ cup) vegetable oil
1 tbsp apple cider vinegar

For the filling
6 tbsp black cherry jam

For the topping
200g (¾ cup) plant-based double cream
2 tbsp caster sugar
Fresh cherries (or tinned)
Dark chocolate, grated

Black Forest cake

Black Forest cake originates from the Black Forest region of Germany, celebrating the region's produce. It's a classic combination of rich chocolate cake, cherries and cream and oh my goodness it's so good!

In my version, the most delicious chocolate cake is filled with cherry jam and topped with whipped plant-based cream, grated chocolate and cherries.

TO MAKE THE CAKE
1. Preheat the oven to 180°C (350°F). Grease and line a loose bottomed cake tin.
2. Mix the dry ingredients in a large bowl.
3. Mix the milk, water, vanilla, vegetable oil and cider vinegar in a jug, then pour into the dry mix.
4. Stir until smooth, then spoon into the lined cake tin.
5. Bake for 35–40 minutes or until a skewer comes out clean from the centre of the cake.
6. Leave to cool, then carefully slice the cake in half.
7. Spoon the cherry jam onto one side of the cake. Place the top on the cake.

TO MAKE THE CREAM
1. Add the cream and sugar to a large bowl.
2. Whisk using a electric whisk or immersion blender until the cream is stiff.
3. Top the cake with the whipped cream and cherries.
4. You can grate some chocolate on top too!
5. Store in the fridge.

INGREDIENTS

Difficulty – Medium
Serves 12
Prep – 1 hr
Cooking – 15 minutes

For the dough

1 tbsp ground flax seeds, plus 3 tbsp water

80g (⅓ cup plus 1 tbsp) caster sugar

180g (12 tbsp/1.5 sticks) vegan butter, room temperature

Pinch sea salt

2 tsp baking powder

260g (2 ⅔ cups) plain flour

Marzipan filling

120g (1 cup) icing sugar

130g (4.5oz) ground almonds

1 tsp almond extract

5 tbsp water

Topping

Whole almonds

Gevulde koeken – marzipan cookies

I think you're going to like these cute little Dutch cookies! And if you adore marzipan like me – you're going to LOVE them. Don't be scared by making the pastry – it's so easy. You just need to add the ingredients to a food processor and blitz. And the marzipan filling is sweet and gorgeous, giving a soft and gooey centre to the crunchy outside.

1. In a jar, mix the ground flaxseed with the water. Set aside.
2. Add the sugar, vegan butter, salt and flaxseed mix to a food processor and blitz to combine.
3. Add the flour and baking powder. Blitz again until you get a soft dough.
4. Transfer to a floured surface and knead the dough for a few minutes.
5. Roll out a little, then wrap in foil and pop in the fridge to firm up for 30–40 minutes.
6. Now make the marzipan filling. Add the icing sugar, ground almonds, almond extract and water to a tub and mix until everything comes together as a thick paste.
7. Preheat the oven to 200°C (400°F).
8. Divide the dough into two, then place the first half onto a floured surface.
9. Roll out the dough to about the thickness of a coin.
10. Using a cookie cutter or the end of a glass. cut 12 rounds. (I use an 8cm wide cutter.)
11. Put 12 rounds on a baking tray lined with parchment paper.
12. Now scoop a heaped tablespoon of the marzipan onto the centre of the dough, and press down gently.
13. Roll out the other half of the dough, cut 12 rounds and place on top.
14. Gently press the edges of the dough together and then press lightly with a fork around the edges.
15. Top with an almond and bake in the oven for 15 minutes, until the cookies are brown.
16. Let the cookies cool before eating.

INGREDIENTS

Difficulty – Medium
Makes 6 crêpes
Prep – 10 minutes
Cooking – 20 minutes

For the crêpes
400ml (1 ⅔ cups) plant-based milk
100ml (⅓ cup plus 1 tbsp) water
250g (1 cup) plain flour
4 tbsp maple syrup
2 tbsp melted coconut or veg oil
1 tsp vanilla extract
1 tsp orange extract
Zest of 1 orange

For the warm strawberries
200g (7oz) strawberries, top removed and sliced in half
2 tbsp light brown sugar
2 tbsp water

For the choc sauce
2 tbsp vegan choc nut spread
3 tbsp water
1 tbsp maple syrup

Toppings
Vegan yoghurt
Maple syrup

French crêpes with warm strawberries & chocolate sauce

Thin and crispy French crêpes are such a treat! The perfect dessert or weekend brunch. Warm strawberries and chocolate sauce are a classic and decadent combination, but you can top with caramelised bananas, sliced oranges, fresh fruit, or peanut butter. Or just keep it simple with a squeeze of lemon juice and maple syrup.

TO MAKE THE CRÊPES
1. In a large bowl mix the crêpe ingredients together with a whisk to remove all the lumps.
2. On a medium heat, add a little oil to a large nonstick frying pan and pour a ladle full of the batter on your pan, move the batter around the pan to spread it thinly.
3. Cook for about 1 min per side, then flip and cook the other side.
4. Remove from the pan, add to a plate and keep them warm under a clean tea towel
5. Repeat with the remaining batter.

FOR THE STRAWBERRIES
Add the strawberries, sugar and water to a small saucepan and heat until just broken down a little.

TO MAKE THE CHOC SAUCE
Add the ingredients to a jar and mix to combine.

TO SERVE
Top with the strawberries, choc sauce, yoghurt and maple.

Caribbean

DRINKS

Japan

India

Europe

For the lassi

160g (⅔ cup) plant-based greek style yoghurt

170g (6oz) ripe mango reeled and sliced - or frozen

½ tsp ginger powder

½ tsp cardamon powder

½ tsp vanilla powder or extract

100ml (⅓ cup plus 1 tbsp) coconut milk drink

1 tbsp maple syrup

Juice ½ lime

Pinch sea salt

Topping ideas

Desiccated coconut

More mango

Fresh mint

Creamy mango & lime lassi

I remember tasting lassi the first time I went to India (way too many years ago now) and loved it. It's traditionally a blend of yoghurt, water and spices – sometimes sweet, sometimes savoury.

My version is made with coconut yoghurt, mango and lots of subtle spices, absolutely gorgeous. Plus I would also absolutely recommend adding some oats and soaking overnight from the most delicious overnight oats.

TO MAKE THE LASSI

1. Add everything to a high speed blender or food processor. Blitz until very creamy.
2. Divide between the glasses, and top with desiccated coconut.

INGREDIENTS

Difficulty – Easy
Serves 2
Prep – 10 minutes

For the shot
150g (5oz) fresh ginger peeled
1 juice lemon
2 oranges
Pinch cayenne pepper

Immune-boosting ginger citrus shot

These firey little ginger and citrus shots are bound to give you a boost!

TO MAKE THE GINGER CITRUS SHOT

1. Peel the ginger, then grate it.
2. Juice the oranges and lemon and add to a jug.
3. Now squeeze the ginger over the jug in the palm of your hand to release the juices.
4. Keep squeezing until the ginger is dry.
5. Mix and divide the juice between two glasses.
6. Top with some cayenne pepper.

Benefits could include
Vitamin C for the immune system,
to help stave off colds
Antioxidants
Maintaining the pH balance of the body
Promoting good oral health

For the latte

2 tsp matcha
2 tsp water
2 tsp maple syrup
100ml (⅓ cup plus 1 tbsp) warm water
200ml (¾ cup) hot or steamed milk

Matcha latte

This delectable delight is a cross between a smoothie and a sorbet, and it's super refreshing. You just blitz the tropical fruits until they're smooth and creamy. It's great as a smoothie or a quick and healthy dessert. If you'd like it less thick, just add some coconut water or plant-based milk.

I also love an iced matcha latte – to make this alternative, add to a tall glass along with lots of ice cubes.

TO MAKE THE MATCHA LATTE

1. Add the matcha to a jug. Mix with 2 tsp of water and the maple syrup.
2. Mix until you get a smooth paste.
3. Warm the milk in the pan until boiling.
4. Now add the warm water and mix to combine.
5. Stir in the milk then divide between two mugs.

Difficulty – Easy
Serves 2 large or 4 small
Prep – 10 minutes

160g (1 cup) frozen
mango chunks
1 passionfruit
100g (½ cup) frozen
pineapple
130g (¾ cup) frozen
bananas

Tropical frozen smoothie

This delectable delight is a cross between a smoothie and a sorbet and super refreshing. Tropical frozen fruits blitzed until smooth and creamy.

Great as a smoothie or a quick and healthy dessert. If you'd like it less thick just add some coconut water or plant based milk.

FOR THE FROZEN SMOOTHIE

Add all ingredients in a blender or food processor and blend until smooth and creamy.

Difficulty – Easy
Serves 2 large or 4 small
Prep – 10 minutes

For the chai spice
1 tbsp. cinnamon
1 tbsp ground cardamom
1 tsp ground ginger
Pinch cloves
½ tsp nutmeg
Pinch black pepper

For chai spice banana smoothie
2 tsp chai spice mixture (above)
250g (9oz) ripe frozen bananas
2 tbsp vegan natural yoghurt
250ml (1 cup) plant-based milk
2 Tbsp peanut or almond butter
1 tsp ground flax seed
1–2 medjool dates pitted

Chai spiced smoothie

A creamy dreamy smoothie made with chai spices, banana and peanut butter.

Masala chai is an Indian tea made with a mixture of black tea, milk and a mixture of aromatic herbs and spices but the gorgeous spice mix is also amazing in desserts and smoothies.

This one is incredibly delicious.

FOR THE CHAI SPICE MIXTURE
Mix all spices together in a small jar.

FOR THE CHAI SMOOTHIE
Add all ingredients in a blender or food processor and blend until smooth and creamy.

Glossary

CRUELTY-FREE

Not tested on animals.

DAIRY-FREE

Contains no dairy products like cow's milk, cheese, butter, yoghurt or cream.

ETHICAL VEGANISM

Ethical vegans are those who don't just eat a plant-based diet, but also oppose the use of animals in any part of their life, including clothing, animal testing and animal labour.

FLEXITARIANISM

A flexitarian is someone who still eats meat and dairy, but is trying to include more plant-based meals in their diet.

PESCETARIANISM

Vegetarians who also eat seafood are known as pescetarians.

PLANT-BASED

A plant-based diet consists of plants including vegetables, fruit, pulses, grains, nuts and seeds. Not necessarily the same as vegan, as some plant products can cause cruelty to animals.

VEGANISM

According to the Vegan Society, "a way of living which seeks to exclude, as far as is possible and practicable, all forms of exploitation of, and cruelty to, animals for food, clothing or any other purpose."

VEGETARIANISM

The practice of avoiding any meat products, including red meat, poultry and seafood. Most vegetarians still eat dairy products like cow's milk and cheese.

TERMS USED

Veganism – Veganism is a way of living which seeks to exclude, as far as is possible and practicable, all forms of exploitation of, and cruelty to, animals for food, clothing or any other purpose.

Plant based – a diet consisting of mostly plants - including; vegetables, fruit, pulses, grains, nuts and seeds.

Cruelty free – means not tested on animals.

Dairy free – contains no dairy products (milk, cheese, butter etc)

Baking powder – A dry leavening agent, used to increase the volume and lighten the texture of baked goods.

Beat – To mix vigorously with a spoon, mixer or spatula Bicarbonate of soda – A mixture of sodium and hydrogen carbonate. When it's mixed with acid (such as vinegar)it creates carbon dioxide which causes the mixture to expand before it's replaced with air.

Blend – To make a liquid using a food processor or blender.

Boil – To heat liquid until it bubbles.

Chop – To cut something into small pieces.

Combine – To mix ingredients together.

Dice – To cut into small cubes.

Dissolve – To melt or liquify something, usually into water.

Drain – To remove excess liquid, using a sieve or colander.

Drizzle – To pour slowly.

Fold – To fold something into a batter without stirring, i.e. choc chips into cake batter.

Grate – To shred into small pieces using a grater.

Grease – To rub oil or spread onto a baking tray or tin to stop sticking.

Harissa – Hot sauce or paste made from chilli pepper, paprika and oil.

Knead – To fold and squash dough repeatedly, to make it more elastic.

Juice – To squeeze liquid out.

Lukewarm – Mildly warm, not hot.

Mince – To chop into extremely small pieces.

Preheat – To turn on the oven so it can reach the correct temperature before cooking or baking.

Pulse – Any food from the legume family, including peas, beans, chickpeas, soybeans and lentils.

Purée – To blend fruit or veg to a thick pulp.

Rinse – To clean by washing under cold water.

Season – To add salt and pepper to dishes to add flavour.

Sauté – To cook/fry in a pan with oil.

SEITAN – Wheat gluten, used to make meat substitutes.

Set – To leave food until it firms up.

Simmer – To heat liquid in a pan on a low heat, until small bubbles rise from it.

Soy – A legume native to east Asia. The bean is used to make soy milk, tofu, soy sauce and tempeh.

Stir fry – To fry rapidly over a high heat, stirring constantly to prevent burning.

Tempeh – A soybean curd, chewier and denser than tofu.

Tofu – A curd made of processed soybeans.

Tahini – Sesame seed paste.

Whip – To beat something to incorporate more air into it.

Whisk – To mix vigorously with a whisk.

Zest – The grated skin of any citrus fruit.

Index

Niki around the
WORLD

Dubai

USA

India

Brazil

Morocco

Caribbean

Thailand
Bali

Israel

India

Spain

Notes

Notes

Notes

Notes

www.rebelrecipes.com
www.instagram.com/rebelrecipes
www.facebook.com/rebelrecipes